VIENNA

 PUBLICATIONS
Part of the Langenscheidt Publishing Group

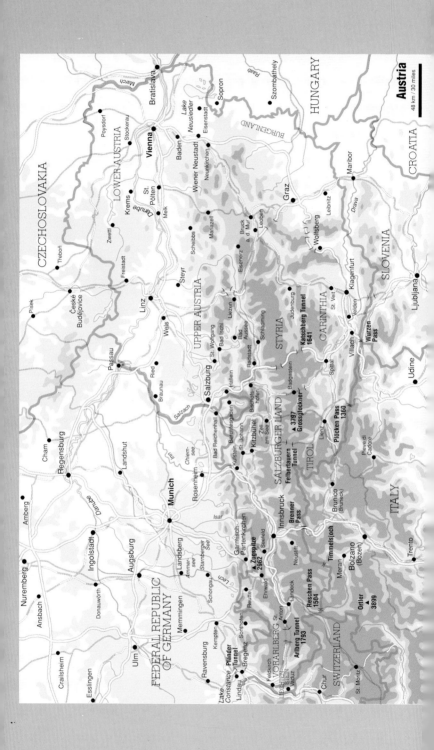

Austria

48 km / 30 miles

Welcome!

This guidebook combines the interests and enthusiasms of two of the world's best-known information providers: Insight Guides, who have set the standard for visual travel guides since 1970, and Discovery Channel, the world's premier source of non-fiction television programming.

At the crossroads of east and west, Vienna is the product of a long and fascinating history. The city has something to offer everyone: great architecture; a world-class opera house and museums; atmospheric coffee-houses and bars; and a beautiful natural setting. In these pages *Insight Guides'* correspondent in Vienna, Nicole Schmidt, has devised a range of itineraries to bring you the best of this diversity. Three full-day tours link essential sights and explore the Old City. They are followed by 13 itineraries ranging from Vienna's art nouveau architecture to excursions into the country-side to sample the *Heuriger* (new wine). Complementing the itineraries are chapters on shopping and eating out, and a practical information section.

 Nicole Schmidt, a journalist in Vienna, is a genuine *Wienerin*, a Viennese woman. She loves her native city, in particular the way it walks a tightrope between old and new. She says romantic images of Sachertorte, waltzes, horse-drawn cabs and getting tipsy on *Heuriger* (new wine) are still alive and well, but adding edge to these soft-focus charms is a lively contemporary scene that is sometimes ignored by guide books. She calls Vienna 'a city that has changed its appearance without actually losing any of its style'. In *Insight Pocket Guide: Vienna* Nicole captures and celebrates all its diverse attractions.

C O N T E N T S

Pages 2/3:
St Stephen's
Cathedral in
winter

J2↓   Linie U3↓

Pages 8/9: ball at the Hofburg

Calendar of Special Events

Shopping and Eating Out

Practical Information

Maps

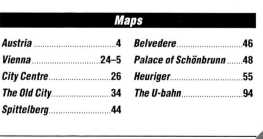

Romans and Habsburgs

Vienna's strategic location on the banks of the Danube has placed it at the centre of the European stage. In 15BC the Romans pitched the military camp of Vindobona on the site of today's District 1. When Leopold I of Babenberg, Heinrich Jasomirgott, moved his seat there in 1155, Vienna quickly developed into a prosperous town at the crossroads of trading routes between east and west and between the Levant, Italy and the north. In the 14th century it became the seat of the Habsburg dynasty, and in 1365 Rudolf IV, the 'Founder', endowed the second university in the German-speaking world, now known as the 'Alte Universität', in Vienna.

In 1529 the Ottoman army attempted to take Vienna but, thanks to an early winter, the city was successfully defended. After this, new fortifications were erected. Remains of these city bastions, which were built in the Renaissance style, are still in existence today (for example, the Mölkerbastei). In the middle of the 16th century Kaiser Ferdinand established the Jesuits in Vienna, who, in the fight against Protestantism, soon had the city's cultural and educational life under control: Vienna developed into a stronghold of Catholicism.

The so-called 'fortress of the Occident' succeeded in withstanding another attack by the Ottoman army in 1683. Afterwards, the rubble that the Turks had left behind in today's suburbs became the foundations of magnificent palaces erected for the nobility by baroque master builders such as Lukas von Hildebrandt and Johann Bernhard Fischer von Erlach. The Upper and Lower Belvederes and the palace of Schönbrunn are among the edifices built at this time. Craftsmen streamed into Vienna from all over the empire, and settled there.

The city's flourishing artistic and cultural life reached its zenith at the beginning of the 18th century. Under the Empress Maria Theresa, Vienna developed its own power base. Her son Joseph II

CULTURE

restrained the power of the Jesuits in favour of the Enlightenment. At the beginning of the 19th century, Napoleon occupied the city; his final defeat was sealed at the Congress of Vienna in 1815.

The Biedermeier Period

The first half of the 19th century is today known as the Biedermeier Period. State Chancellor Metternich, with his secret police, presided over everything from the Ballhausplatz, and *'der gute Kaiser Franz'*, who considered any form of new idea inherently suspect, was entrenched in the Hofburg. Perhaps no epoch has seemed so cliché-ridden in retrospect as the period between the festive Congress of Vienna and the burning barricades of 1848, the year of revolutions throughout Europe: superficially it was characterised by the emergence of a middle class carried away on crazes for operetta, the waltz, floral wallpaper, beer and sausages.

The comfortable middle classes were not as naive as all that, though: they could see that within the straitjacket of the police

Historical Vienna

The Meat Market

state contrary forces were at work. Just as much a part of the Biedermeier period were Beethoven's rebellious genius, Ferdinand Raimund's amusing magic theatre and Peter Fendi's 'pornographic' drawings. The prevailing mood was a tension between extreme subservience on one hand, and on the other the satirical rebelliousness of, for example, Johann Nestroy. And while all this was going on, the age of the steam engine and of proletarian revolt was dawning.

In March 1848, bloody revolution broke out. Townspeople, workers and students all rose up against repression. Metternich and the royal family fled; they retaliated, however, as early as October. By the end of 1848, the 18-year-old Franz Joseph's accession to the throne was proclaimed. The beginning of his reign was marked by a period of neo-absolutism.

In 1857 Franz Joseph had the old defensive walls torn down to make way for the expanding city. The walls were replaced by Vienna's magnificent Ringstrasse. The *Gründerzeit* epoch, Vienna's great expansion, was at its height. Architects and builders moved into Vienna from all over Europe, turning it into a melting-pot once again. Building styles also blended into each other. Historicism was all the rage: the Opera House and the new Burgtheater were built in a mixture of neoclassical and Italian Renaissance styles, the Town Hall was given Neo-Gothic towers, and the Parlament (parliament building) was built in the Greek Revival style.

The exciting atmosphere of the *Gründerzeit* also affected municipal policy. In 1860 Vienna had its first ever Liberal mayor, and Otto Wagner's *Jugendstil* buildings (the Viennese version of *art nouveau*) such as the Secession Building and the Postsparkasse (Post Office Savings Bank), set new trends in architecture.

This boom in investment soon turned to bust, however: the working class lived in miserable conditions, and a cholera epidemic and a stock exchange crash put an end to the economic boom as well as the Vienna World Fair. This recession was a home-made one, at least in part. Technologically, Vienna was limping behind most other cities. Its *petite bourgeoisie* was concentrating on the struggle against industry and finance, and took refuge in anti-semitic feeling. Very soon all the pomp and finery was riddled with corruption. At the same time, however, art and philosophy flourished as never before under figures such as Gustav Klimt and Otto Wagner, Adolf Loos and Josef Hoffmann, Sigmund Freud and Arthur Schnitzler. Vienna's Jewish community provided the city with that famous *fin de siècle* culture that the world still talks about today.

Racism and Fascism

In 1895 Karl Lueger ('I decide who's Jewish and who isn't'), representing the anti-capitalist *petite bourgeoisie*, was voted mayor of Vienna. The Austro-Hungarian Empire was teetering on the brink of collapse, and its various subject peoples were seething with discontent. The assassination of the successor to the throne, Franz Ferdinand, was a welcome excuse – rather than the real reason – for World War I. In 1916 Emperor Franz Joseph died after 68 years in power. His grand-nephew Karl was forced to leave the country at the end of the war and the Austro-Hungarian Empire came apart at the seams. Suddenly, Vienna was nothing more than the self-important centre of a giant administrative system that had ceased to exist.

Universal suffrage, introduced in 1919, gave the Social Democrats the majority in the Gemeindeparlament (City Parliament). 'Red Vienna', as it was now called, set up kindergartens and exemplary housing projects such as the Karl-Marx-Hof, which is still considered a milestone in public-assistance housing even today. Alongside all this, however, the seed of Fascism was steadily growing. Seemingly irreconcilable differences between the Christian Socialists and the Social Democrats led to shooting in the streets and finally, in 1934, to civil war. The Austro-Fascist regime under Engelbert Dollfuss took over.

In 1938 Hitler annexed Austria with much popular approval, though many opposition groups, including Jews and artists, were forced to flee or were deported and murdered. Before World War II there were 170,000 Jews in Vienna; today there are around 6,000. In April 1945 the Red Army liberated Vienna and the Allies divided the city into four zones of occupation. One-fifth of Vienna's houses had been destroyed, and the Opera House and the roof of St Stephen's Cathedral were in flames.

Several of the former rival politicians from the Social Democratic Party (now called the SPÖ) and the Christian Socialist Party (now the ÖVP) had spent time with one another in concentration camps, and being in the same boat made them decide to forget their old differences. With diplomatic skill, Austria

Rooftiles of St Stephen's Cathedral

Historical Highlights

5000BC First traces of human settlement in Vienna.

15BC The Emperor Augustus conquers the kingdom of Noricum, the area of present-day Vienna.

AD100 The Romans set up the military garrison of Vindobona as defence against the Germanic tribes; a town grows up around it.

5th century The Huns conquer Vienna; the Roman Empire collapses, Roman troops leave Vindobona.

881 First mention of Vienna.

10th century Emperor Otto I names the region a frontier area of his kingdom against the East.

1137 Vienna is granted municipal status.

1155 Vienna becomes the seat of the Babenberg dynasty.

1282 Habsburg rule begins.

1359 Rudolf IV, the 'Founder', lays the foundation stone for the Gothic nave of St Stephen's Cathedral.

1365 Vienna University – the second university in the German-speaking world – is founded.

1438 Vienna becomes a residency.

1529 First Turkish siege; the city is refortified in following decades.

Mid-16th century The Reformation also reaches Vienna.

1577 Jesuits 'recatholicise' Vienna.

1679 Plague causes havoc.

1683 Second Turkish siege.

1740 Maria Theresa becomes Empress.

1766 The Prater is opened to the general public.

1805/9 Napoleonic occupation.

1814–15 Congress of Vienna.

1848 A popular uprising overthrows Metternich; Emperor Franz Joseph takes the throne.

1857 The city's old defensive walls are knocked down; construction work begins on the Ringstrasse.

1865 Festive opening ceremony for a section of the Ringstrasse.

1873 The World Fair is a failure due to the stock exchange crash and a cholera epidemic.

1896 The giant Ferris Wheel is installed in the Prater.

1914 Murder of Franz Ferdinand in Sarajevo triggers World War I.

1916 Emperor Franz Joseph dies, his grand-nephew Karl takes over.

1918 The Austro-Hungarian monarchy collapses; the Emperor leaves Austria; on 12 November the first republic is declared.

1919 Universal suffrage introduced; the Social Democrats rule Vienna.

1922 Vienna becomes an independent federal state in its own right.

1934 Civil war between Social Democrats and Christian Socialists.

1938 Hitler annexes Austria.

1945 The Red Army liberates Vienna; the city is divided into four zones of occupation.

15 May 1955 State Treaty signed.

26 October 1955 Permanent neutrality approved by Austrian constitutional law (a national holiday).

1961 Kennedy/Krushchev summit.

1969 Construction work begins on the city's U-Bahn system.

1979 UN-City opened. Vienna becomes the third most important UN centre. Brezhnev/Carter summit.

1986–9 4th KSZE (European Security and Cooperation Conference).

August 1991 Austria starts negotiations to join the EU.

1 January 1995 Austria becomes a member of the EU.

February 2000 The People's Party forms a coalition with the right-wing Freedom Party. This results in protest in Austria and abroad and in the temporary isolation of the country from the rest of the EU.

won back its independence. On 15 May 1955 Federal Chancellor Figl waved the signed State Treaty *(Staatsvertrag)* from the balcony of the Belvedere.

Reconstruction could now continue with renewed vigour. But the threat posed by the proximity of the Iron Curtain was ever-present. People took refuge in a form of apathy, and the whole country fell into a post-imperial torpor. Renewed self-confidence was slow in coming; after the initial euphoria at the collapse of the Iron Curtain had subsided it seemed for a while as if the old anxiety was returning. In 1990 there were sudden calls for compulsory visas and drastic cuts in immigration. The flames of anti-foreigner sentiment are being fanned by the far-right wing Freedom Party (FPÖ) under Jörg Haider, whose embarrassing political rise has created a national image problem.

Vienna has spent a long time indulging in its undisputed function as a bridgehead for contact with the East; now that the term 'Central Europe' is becoming widely accepted it is going to have to redefine its position and 'compete' anew with Prague and Budapest, its rivals during Empire days. This is one reason why Austrians voted to join the EU in 1994. It is a challenge for the new millennium, and one that can only do the city good.

The Viennese Character

One disadvantage of clichés is that they deprive you of your free, unprejudiced view of things, and automatically affect your later impressions; an advantage they do have, though, is that they can act as a sort of guide through forests of false appearances. The Viennese character is a mixture of noisy self-confidence and inferiority complexes – the self-satisfied *Mir san mir* ('we are who we are') attitude, the sense of having once been the centre of the world, mingled with the shock of having suddenly been pushed onto the sidelines of Europe.

The disappearance of the Iron Curtain has created a whole new set of problems, because such change brings competition in its wake. Suddenly Prague and Budapest, the city's former rivals, which it had successfully upstaged for so long, are back in the running. And fair competition has never been one of Vienna's strong points.

The Viennese prefer to day-dream about change than to welcome it when it happens. 'Things have always been that way.' They grumble about the status quo, but there again, they've adapted to it very nicely. Change is considered

One of Vienna's eccentrics

troublesome and only ever really gets acknowledged once it's over and done with. Until the new becomes properly old, makeshift solutions apply. Things can always be better assimilated in retrospect: Beethoven has become an Austrian, Hitler a German, and the enormous cheering crowd that welcomed the Nazi leader on the Heldenplatz in 1938 is forgotten. Conflicts have remained unresolved.

Hardly any city in the world has contributed more to 20th-century thought than Vienna, and hardly any city has shown itself less appreciative of its creative and intellectual elite. People such as architects Otto Wagner and Adolf Loos, the artists Klimt and Schiele, writers Werfel and Musil, as well as Freud, Schönberg, Wittgenstein, Karl Kraus and Josef Hoffmann: Vienna likes to boast of these names today. Unfortunately, such great Viennese artists and thinkers have had to be acknowledged outside Austria first before gaining acceptance there, and their current popularity is only retrospective. Comedian Helmut Qualtinger summed it up: 'In Vienna you need to die before you become popular, but once you're dead you live a long time.'

As time goes by, this rejection of anything new gradually turns into parochial approval. For example, buildings that were once the object of passionate dispute, such as the Opera House or the Loos House, are now old enough to be shown off proudly, while contemporary Viennese architects such as Hans Hollein, Gustav Peichl or Wilhelm Holzbauer are forced to do most of their work abroad. Until recently the sum total of Hollein's work in Vienna was a few shop fronts. His Haas-Haus on the Stephansplatz was only given building permission once the mayor had given his approval – 'beer-hall critics' regard anything modern at all in the heart of the city as blasphemy. In 100 years' time, though, the Viennese will probably be as proud of their Hollein as they are of their Opera House today.

Having to make continual compromises can often be intellectually rewarding, but it's when one's patience is finally at an end that the leap to greatness is often achieved and a brilliant mind steps out of the shadows that it seemed to need in order to shine. That's Viennese dialectics for you. It is no coincidence that Vienna was the place where Musil produced his novel *The Man Without Qualities*, and Freud developed psychoanalysis.

The essence of Vienna is contradiction; fantasy and reality aren't real opposites here at all. In the opinion of the late author György Sebestyén: 'Since there's apparently no distinction between reality and game-playing, it's better to treat reality as a game than vice-versa. And when reality becomes just as senseless as its 'game version', then the game at least has to be cheerful: after all, it costs the same, and we're all going to die anyway.'

'*Verkauft's mei G'wand, i fahr in Himmel*' ('I'm off to heaven – sell my clothes') says the fatalistic Viennese, and retreats to the inner sanctuary of his soul along with his deep fried chicken and his wine – for after all, '*Es wird a Wein sein, und wir wer'n nimmer sein*' ('we're all going to die, so let's have another wine').

The Viennese are inveterate grumblers. It's a form of rebellion against 'them up there', cultivated over centuries of being dominated by the imperial court. They mock, certainly, but in the end they always pull themselves together and bow to authority: *Meine Verehrung* (reverence), *Herr Hofrat* (*Hofrat* is the rough equivalent of a Privy Councillor).

The imperial court has long since disappeared, but its heritage remains, and titles are still all-important. The genuine *Hofrat* proudly wears his title as the shining badge of his rather tedious work as a civil servant; any *Hofrat* who isn't a genuine one is thought of far less highly. Ordinary teachers in Vienna are addressed as *Professor*, which is why real university professors always stick a *univ* in front of their title. Their respective wives are addressed, even in local grocery shops, as *Frau Professor* or *Frau Medizinalrat* regardless of whether or not they possess a title of their own. In business life one has to be a *Kommerzialrat* at least; the best way to inspire respect among your fellow Viennese is to refer to yourself as *k.u.k. Hoflieferant* (roughly: 'purveyor to the Royal Court') and sport the Habsburg double-headed eagle on your letterheads.

But even nostalgia for the double-headed eagle is not without its share of complications, especially when it comes to the Austrians' former compatriots from the East. They're quite happy to have tourists visit their country, but would rather have as little as possible to do with *Ausländer* (foreigners), even though the typical inhabitant of Vienna is a superb Central European mixture of a Bohemian grandmother, a Polish aunt and a Levantine merchant – and proud of it.

'*Das Boot ist voll*' (the boat is full) was the SPÖ's former general secretary's response a few years ago to the rise in immigration from the East. The gentleman in question's surname happened to be Marizzi, and his colleague's name was Cap. Recent governments, whose members have names such as Vranitzky, Klima and Lacina,

Reflecting on the past

Dohnal and Busek, are proof enough of how the Viennese became Viennese in the first place.

The Viennese are notoriously contradictory in their rejection of foreigners. They complain about *die Ausländer* – and the fewer foreigners they know, the louder they'll complain – but at the same time they'll leap to the defence of their Polish cleaning ladies. They'll look down condescendingly on *die Fremden* (strangers) and simultaneously fight to keep a kebab shop on their street corner in business. But beneath the distrust, the melancholy and the grumbling you'll also find a sharp wit, and a talent for improvisation and adaptation. Some people reckon that it was this ability to walk the wobbly tightrope of diplomacy plus all the wine, charm and Viennese *schmäh* that led to the country gaining its freedom in 1955.

Granted, it did take over 20 years for the intelligentsia finally to rebel and overcome the *petit bourgeois* fustiness of the post-war era, and create a new cultural and gastronomic scene – but Vienna is the envy of a lot of other cities as a result. The provincial attitudes one encounters in some parts of the city are still a major obstacle, but so is the all-too-easy escape into the faceless anonymity of a large metropolis.

'Now don't get all matter-of-fact – you can remain personal', as Anton Kuh once put it. If you're good at it, Vienna is the perfect venue for noisy, self-confident show-offs. Anyone without any egocentric ambitions who feels threatened by the meaninglessness of it all can always retreat into their inner sanctuaries and console themselves with Georg Hauptfeld's phrase: 'An intentional lie often comes closer to the truth than the truth itself, which is always doubtful.' *Wien ist anders* (Vienna is different) was the cheerful message of the city's official advertising campaign. Now it's *Wien bleibt Wien* (Vienna remains Vienna), which was ominously pronounced by Karl Kraus. The truth probably lies – quite typically for Vienna – somewhere between the two.

Theatre and Music

Anyone who mentions theatre in Vienna is usually thinking of the Burgtheater and Max Reinhardt. The fact that a *Piefke* (derogatory word for a German) in the shape of Claus Peymann called the shots from 1986 until 1999 at the 'Burg', as the theatre is affectionately termed, has left several deep wounds in many a Vienna theatregoer. Be that as it may, Mr Peymann has still succeeded in shaking this theatre out of its former complacency. Vienna, unusually, is a city in which the actors at the 'Burg' have the status of civil servants, and premières still provoke scandals – such as Thomas Bernhard's *Heldenplatz*, aimed directly

Vienna Opera House

at the darkest recesses of the Viennese soul, or Peter Turrini's *Death and the Devil*, at the première of which state police could be seen scribbling away in the stalls, noting down the scenes that might cause offence. Theatre in Vienna is definitely a stimulating experience. Yet at the same time, most of the small theatre groups are fighting for their survival. The Serapionstheater, with its fantastic, pantomime-like theatre collages, deserves a special mention in this category.

As proud denizens of what is, after all, the 'capital city of music', the Viennese are also concerned about the Opera. And whenever they aren't queueing all night for tickets, equipped with a small folding chair, they are happily sawing away at the legs of the chair of the opera director, who has the most dangerous job in the whole city. The repertoire can vary a great deal in quality, as can the cast – but historic moments still occur. (A useful tip: the best way to get hold of tickets is either to order them in writing from abroad or else discreetly ask the head porter of your hotel.)

The Opera House only really makes a large profit once a year: on the night of the Opera Ball, when the city's *jeunesse dorée* waltzes inside the building and the Opera Ball Demo takes place outside on the street. The latter has practically become an institution. And while on the subject of tradition; anyone who likes hearing operetta and goes to the Volksoper is definitely at the right place. Even the city's critics are fond of the Vienna Philharmonic, especially its annual New Year Concert on 1 January in the Great Hall of the Musikverein, which is broadcast right across the world.

Display case at the Burgtheater

Waltzes played in the gardens of baroque palaces, organ concerts in old churches or classical music and jazz in the Arkadenhof in the Town Hall are all part of the variety provided by the Wiener Musiksommer (July and August), and in May and June the Wiener Festwochen brighten the cultural life of the city with international performances ranging from the traditional to the avant-garde. Since the musical *Cats* arrived here, Vienna has thought of itself as home to this particular art-form as well – judge for yourself at the Theater an der Wien.

Of course there's comedy in Vienna too, but its return to the city has been comparatively recent. The legendary cabaret scene of the post-war era with Karl Farkas, Ernst Waldbrunn or Helmut Qualtinger has only borne fruit in the past 15 to 20 years or so. Now there are not only young cabaret performers such as Lukas Resetarits,

Josef Hader, Erwin Steinhauer or Andreas Vitasek, but also the cabaret venues to go with them, such as the Kulisse, the Metropol, the Spektakel or the Niedermair.

Politics and Population

Ever since universal suffrage was introduced in 1919, Vienna has been ruled by the Socialist Party of Austria (SPÖ) with almost 50 percent of the vote; they were only absent from the Gemeinderat (municipal parliament) between 1934 and 1945. Since the recent elections, the Green Party and the right-wing FPÖ have been represented in the Town Hall for the first time. Nowhere else is the network of party members so close-woven: of 1.6 million Viennese, nearly 200,000 are members of the SPÖ and more than 50,000 members of the Austrian People's Party (ÖVP). This does not have to do exclusively with 'red' (SPÖ) and 'black' (ÖVP) political leanings, for the importance of party goes much further than this. Until recently, when a massive privatisation programme of formerly state-run companies was launched, the state provided a great many jobs on the basis of 'colour' rather than qualifications, and to a certain extent it still does.

The same goes for the whole of Austria of course, but Vienna is ahead of everywhere else in this respect. Take the *Freunderlwirtschaft* (Vienna's special version of nepotism), for example: everyone knows a civil servant or a functionary who can get the person in charge of a department or institution to do a favour, whether it involves obtaining a theatre ticket, or securing a council flat.

Important laws and decisions get *ausgschnapst* (discussed at a game of cards) before they reach parliament, by the so-called *Sozialpartnerschaft* (the employers' and employees' association). The expression *ausgschnapst* comes from the card game of the same name, and is a highly official term. Here a balance of interests is established without the need to 'bother' the people or their representatives with any problems. Admittedly, the employers' and employees' association has brought social peace to Austria and some of the lowest strike figures worldwide, but it has also resulted in a huge amount of shady dealing. 'For some mysterious reason, the Laocoön-like clutches in which all public figures are held bring a black scandal along to match every red one,' as Armin Thurnherr, editor-in-chief of the critical city magazine *Falter*, once put it. There is, so to speak, a 'balance of detection'.

The people have very little say in these matters. And reforms are always instigated from above in Vienna anyway. The Viennese are thoroughly versed in the role of the underdog. It's only when their anger finally boils over that the dam bursts – to everyone's amazement. As Emperor Ferdinand I said in great surprise when the revolution of 1848 broke out: *'Ja derfen's denn des?'* ('but – do they have permission?').

Civic autonomy has only recently started to wake up, and for a long time was confined to small protest groups and signature-collecting on issues such as *Baummord* (tree murder) and traffic congestion. The prevailing attitude is usually as follows: there'll be no underground car park in front of *my* house, the traffic can roar through the street next door, etc.

All else that need be said here is that the security officials and police in Vienna have a great deal of power; the unemployment rate is low compared with other European cities; that the city's prisons are rather full in comparison to many other European countries; and that there are 9,000 associations, 60,000 dogs and over 300 sausage stalls. After 10pm every fourth Viennese is already tucked up in bed, and every second one creeps out of it as early as 6am to go to work.

Statistics are well known for the way they sometimes shed light on peculiarities.

Inside the Town Hall

Orientation

Although Vienna is clearly laid out, newcomers often have trouble getting their bearings because of the numerous one-way streets. Imagine a huge cake with St Stephen's Cathedral towering over it in the middle. Around it are the small streets of District 1 (1. Bezirk), surrounded by the Ringstrasse and the Donaukanal. Originally, Vienna only occupied today's District 1, and until the 1860s the city wall followed the course of the Ringstrasse. A Viennese referring to the *Stadt* (town) usually means District 1.

The large arterial roads then spread out from the Ring in star formation towards the city's outer districts. On the border between what used to be the edge of the city proper and the suburbs runs the second ring around Vienna, the Gürtel, a dual-carriageway that looks like a ring-road. The so-called *Zweierlinie* (made up of Landesgerichtsstrasse and Lastenstrasse) between the Town Hall and the Karlsplatz runs parallel to the Ring.

If you arrive from the Westautobahn (A1), follow the signs saying *Zentrum*; this way you reach the Karlsplatz via the Wiental, and then you can go left to the Opera House on the Ring. Here you have to turn off left in the direction of the Parlament, because it's a one-way system. From the Südautobahn (A2) the best way of reaching the centre is to follow Triesterstrasse as far as the Gürtel, and then go down Schönbrunnerstrasse, which takes you to the Wienzeile just before the Karlsplatz. Anyone coming from the Danube Valley *(Donautal)* – from the Wachau for example – would do best to follow the Nordautobahn (A22) over the Nordbrücke and then go along the Donaukanal as far as Schwedenplatz.

If you're arriving by car from the airport – 17 km (10½ miles) southeast of the city – take the Flughafenautobahn in the direction of the city centre and when you get to the Urania, turn left over the Donaukanal to reach the Ring.

Driving yourself around the city centre is not recommended; even the locals get lost in the perpetually changing maze of one-ways. Kärntnerstrasse, Graben, Kohlmarkt and all the smaller streets around them are pedestrian precincts. Within the Ringstrasse everything can be comfortably reached on foot. The most important sights are all in District 1: along the Ringstrasse are the Opera House, the Parlament, the Burgtheater, the Town Hall, the Alte Universität and Otto Wagner's Post Office Savings Bank, not to mention the Museum of Fine Arts and Natural History.

The two main stations are both on the Gürtel: the Südbahnhof, at the end of Prinz-Eugen-Strasse, which leads off the Schwarzenbergplatz, and the Westbahnhof, at the end of Mariahilferstrasse.

Vienna is divided up into 23 administrative districts, or *Bezirke*; around the centre, between the Ring and the Gürtel, are districts 2 to 9, with districts 10 to 23 outside the Gürtel. Each district has its own four-digit postal code, with a '1' placed at the beginning of the district's number, and a '0' at the end: eg '1010' would be District 1.

Vienna

320 m / 0.2 miles

Exploring the City's Heart

From Stephansplatz through the narrow streets of the Old Town to the Opera House. Evening meal at Oswald & Kalb or at Reinhard Gerer's Korso.

– U1/U3 to Stephansplatz –

Begin at the heart of the city, or, to be more precise, beneath its heart. Deep down in the U-Bahn station **Stephansplatz**, shortly before the station exit (signposted 'Stephansplatz'), the shiny chrome

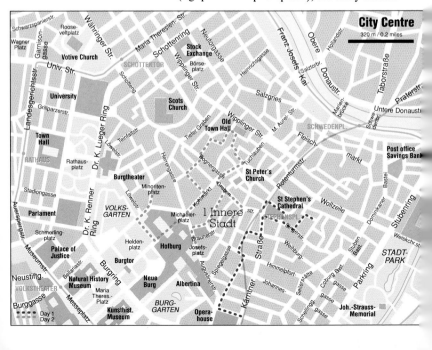

City Centre

320 m / 0.2 miles

Schwarzspanierstr.

Rooseveltplatz

Wagner Platz

Garnisongasse

Währinger Str.

Maria Theresien- Str.

Schottenring

Neutorgasse

Heinrichsgasse

Franz Josefs- Kai

Salztorbr.

Obere Donaust.

Hollardstr.

Taborstraße

Votive Church

SCHOTTENTOR

Univ. Str.

Wippinger Str.

Stock Exchange

Börseplatz

Salzgries

Marienbrücke

Schwedenbr.

Praterstr.

Untere Donaustr.

Landesgerichtsstr.

Schottengasse

University

Grillparzerstr.

Dr. K. Lueger Ring

Teinfaltstr.

Scots Church

Tiefer Graben

Old Town Hall

Wippinger Str.

M. Aurel-Str.

Fleisch-

SCHWEDENPL.

RATHAUS

Town Hall

Löwelstr.

Herrengasse

Bognergasse

Tuchlauben

Rotenturmstr.

markt

Post office Savings Bank

Rathausplatz

Burgtheater

Minoritenplatz

Kohlmarkt

Graben

St Peter's Church

Bastei

Stadiongasse

Löwelstr.

VOLKS-GARTEN

Michaelerplatz

1 Innere Stadt

str.

St Stephen's Cathedral

STEPHANSPL.

Singerstr.

Wollzeile

Dominikaner

Stubenring

Parlament

Dr. K. Renner Ring

Schmerlingplatz

Heldenplatz

Hofburg

Braunerstr.

Josefsplatz

Spiegelgasse

Weihburg-

Weiskschr.st.

Auerspergstr.

Museumstr.

Bellariastr.

Burgring

Burgtor

Neue Burg

Albertina

Augustinerstr.

Kärntner

Straße

Himmelpfort.

Johannes-

Seilerstätte

Coburg Bast.

STADT-PARK

Parkring

Palace of Justice

Burgtheater

Neustiftg.

VOLKSTHEATER

Burggasse

Messeplatz

Natural History Museum

Maria Theres.-Platz

Kunsthist. Museum

BURG-GARTEN

Opera-house

Schenkengb. gasse

Schellinggasse

Joh.-Strauss-Memorial

Day 1
Day 2

The Haas-Haus

walkway ends in front of a thick wall of glass with the vaulted ceiling of **St Virgil's Chapel** illuminated behind it.

The late Romanesque entrance of the **cathedral** (the so-called *Riesentor* or 'Giant Portal') was consecrated in the year 1147. Towering above its left flank is the 'most finely conceived tower of the Gothic period', the 137-m (450-ft) high Südturm, or South Tower, referred to by the Viennese as the *Steffl*. Access to the Nordturm (North Tower), via a lift, is in the left side-aisle (summer: daily 9am–6pm; winter: daily 8.30am–5pm); access to the Südturm on the right outer side of the cathedral (daily 9am–5.30pm). The Südturm has the better view of Vienna's many rooftop-gardens, if you can brave the 343 narrow steps. On the Nordturm, however, you can wonder at the 21-tonne 'Pummerin', the great bell cast from Turkish cannons in the early 18th century. (The time of the next guided tour of the cathedral is posted at the start of the left side-aisle.)

Only two Gothic masterpieces have remained intact inside the triple-naved cathedral with its baroque additions: the magnificent Wiener Neustädter Altar (next to the baroque high altar) and the pulpit. Under its winding staircase, the sculptor Meister Anton Pilgram immortalised himself in a half-figure self-portrait looking through a window. A few metres further on, a stairway leads down to the **catacombs**. They contain the Herzogsgruft, a vault where the Habsburg family used to preserve their relatives' innards in bronze boxes. (Guided tours of the catacombs: Monday to Saturday 10–11.30am and 1–4pm; Sunday, Public Holidays: 1.30–4.30pm.)

On the left of the cathedral, the famous *fiaker* (the name given in Vienna to the horse-drawn cabs as well as to their drivers) are waiting for customers. A trip on these traditional two-horse vehicles can be romantic, but always settle on a fixed price before departing.

On the other side of the cathedral, on the corner of Stephansplatz and the Graben, is the round glass facade of the **Haas-Haus**. It's a harmonious mix of Gothic and 20th-century styles. Inside this architectural symphony of colourful marble, shining brass and cool glass is a three-storey atrium with expensive shops. From the café on the 7th floor you can get the best view of the Cathedral's colourful roof tiles while you sip a coffee and enjoy a slice of *Domspitz*, a special triangular cake with plum jam, poppy seeds and chocolate. Behind the cathedral, at No 4 Stephansplatz, take the passageway next to the attractive teashop Haas & Haas to reach an old-style Viennese inner courtyard: wild vines climb up the bright white facades, a pergola arches over white wicker furniture; it is an oasis of tranquillity in the middle of the city. In the adjacent courtyard a stone statue between two oleander bushes peers down at the paving-stones.

A passageway opposite will lead you to the **Singerstrasse**, site of the church and treasury of the Deutscher Orden, the Teutonic knights. Next door, the frescoed **Sala Terena** is a tiny concert hall with the world's best acoustics, if we are to believe the ticket pedlars who roam the area in period costume. A left on the Singerstrasse and another left on Blutgasse take you to the **Domgasse**, a quiet, winding street, where time seems to stand still. Wolfgang Amadeus Mozart lived at No 5, the **Figaro-Haus** (daily except Monday 9am–6pm) from 1784–87, and it was here that he wrote *The Marriage of Figaro*.

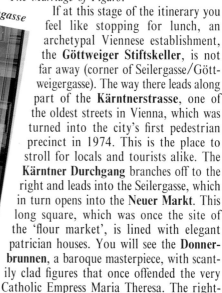

Window display in the Liliengasse

If at this stage of the itinerary you feel like stopping for lunch, an archetypal Viennese establishment, the **Göttweiger Stiftskeller**, is not far away (corner of Seilergasse/Göttweigergasse). The way there leads along part of the **Kärntnerstrasse**, one of the oldest streets in Vienna, which was turned into the city's first pedestrian precinct in 1974. This is the place to stroll for locals and tourists alike. The **Kärntner Durchgang** branches off to the right and leads into the Seilergasse, which in turn opens into the **Neuer Markt**. This long square, which was once the site of the 'flour market', is lined with elegant patrician houses. You will see the **Donnerbrunnen**, a baroque masterpiece, with scantily clad figures that once offended the very Catholic Empress Maria Theresa. The right-hand corner of the Neuer Markt is dominated by the red-brown facade of the **Kapuzinerkirche**, which includes the **Kaisergruft**, the Habsburg burial vault since the early 17th century.

Hot snacks and salads behind a wonderful *Jugendstil* facade can be enjoyed at the **Führich**, in the Führichgasse which leads off the Tegetthoffstrasse, an extension of the Neuer Markt that opens out into **Albertinaplatz**, where sculptor Alfred Hrdlicka erected his *Monument against War and Fascism*, depicting an elderly Jew cleaning the street with a brush

The Hotel Sacher

On the left is the magnificent **Opera House** (Staatsoper), a structure compared by the Viennese to 'an elephant lying down to digest' at its opening in 1869. A mixture of Romanesque, Gothic and Renaissance styles, the building, designed by architects Eduard van der Nüll and August von Sicardsburg, was not to popular taste. Van der Nüll committed suicide before the building was opened, and von Siccardsburg died of a broken heart.

Directly opposite the Opera House, the **Albertina** contains the largest collection of graphic art in the world, and the nearby **Augustinerbastei**, once a secret entrance to the Hofburg, affords a magnificent view of the green copper roof of the Opera House and the Burggarten. Behind the Opera House, in the Philharmonikerstrasse, is the traditional **Hotel Sacher**; it will send its world-famous cake to you wherever you live (for a considerable fee).

In the evening you can either indulge in some Viennese *nouvelle cuisine* created by Reinhard Gerer, one of the city's highly decorated chefs, in his **Restaurant Korso** in the Mahlerstrasse, or retire to one of Vienna's best-known *Edelbeisl* (upper-class tavern), **Oswald & Kalb**. Its comfortable vaulted room in the Bäckerstrasse is a meeting-place for all kinds of writers, politicians and artists. Specialities are *Gefüllte Kalbsbrust* (stuffed veal), *Tafelspitz* (boiled fillet of beef) and, of course, *Wiener Schnitzel*.

The courtyard at Haas & Haas

Imperial Vienna

A stroll through the Vienna of the Habsburgs, the Romans and the Babenbergs; to a traditional pastry shop and café; evening meal in an old-fashioned Viennese 'Edelbeisl', and a nightcap in Vienna's finest 'Plüschbar'.

– U3 to Herrengasse or taxi to Ballhausplatz or Minoritenplatz –

Only a few steps away from the bustling business streets of the city, the **Minoritenplatz** is a tranquil oasis where the only sound is of footsteps resounding on its cobblestones. In the centre of the square is the 700-year-old **Basilica of the Minorites**. In the direction of the Heldenplatz you can see the rear of **Ballhausplatz**. The magnificent Federal Chancellery building on this square was constructed in 1717 by Lukas von Hildebrandt; Metternich once used to pull his political strings here, and the Congress of Vienna also took place within its walls.

Leave the Ballhausplatz on your right and enter the spacious Heldenplatz in front of the Hofburg, the former centre of imperial power and government, sadly damaged by fire in 1992. The equestrian statues of Prince Eugene and Archduke Karl dominate the square. The one of Karl is the only equestrian statue in the world to have its full weight resting on just one hoof. At the front end of the Heldenplatz is the majestic **Neue Burg**, with the National-bibliothek (National Library) behind its immense colonnade.

Follow the clattering hooves of the *fiakers* over to the left and through the gate into the **Hofburg**. On the right-hand side is the oldest part of the Hofburg, the **Alte Burg** (or Old Palace). Its

Fiaker on the Heldenplatz

The Demel confectionery

magnificent dark-red portal leads to the Swiss Court, or Schweizer Hof, and the Treasury (Schatzkammer), where the 1,000-year-old imperial crown of the Holy Roman Empire, the treasures of the Burgundians and the heirlooms of the Habsburgs are displayed

Go past the Reichskanzleitrakt, the seat of the Federal President, and the next gateway will lead you into the Michaelertrakt, crowned by the impressive Michaeler Dome. To the right, a stairway leads up to the former Imperial Chambers.

Now step out of the Hofburg into the Michaelerplatz. The remains of some ancient walls, dating back to Roman times, were discovered in the centre of the square at the beginning of the 1990s. On the left side of the square is the resurrected **Café Griensteidl**, which serves excellent breakfasts.

Opposite the Michaeler Dome, the pedestrian precinct of the **Kohlmarkt** begins, flanked by the **Michaelerkirche** and the **Loos-Haus**. The latter building, constructed by Adolf Loos in 1911, was mocked by the Viennese as a 'house without eyebrows' (because the windows didn't have lintels) and a 'marble coal scuttle'; the Emperor in the Hofburg opposite is said to have shifted his office to other rooms to avoid the 'unbearable sight'. Today the Loos-Haus is considered a milestone of modern architecture.

The Kohlmarkt is one of the most elegant shopping streets in Vienna. Shops belonging to former *k.u.k. Hoflieferanten* ('purveyors to the Imperial Court') throng its sides. After passing the *Kammeruhrmacher* (imperial watchmaker) Franz Morawetz and the elegant displays of Christofle and Kiss & Rosza, you come face-to-face with a favourite Viennese institution: the **Hofkonditorei Demel** – a traditional pastry shop staffed by black-clad waitresses, called *Demelinarinnen*, who address their guests in the third person. Inside you will find all manner of calorie-laden confectionery: cakes, wonderfully packed sweets, and delicious specialities. At the end of the 1980s the Demel had a spot of unwelcome publicity when its then owner, the designer Udo Proksch, was implicated in a murderous scheme to swindle an insurance company by deliberately sinking the freighter *Lucona*. These days – much to the horror of tradition-conscious Viennese – the shop belongs to a German industrialist. But Vienna's imperial past lives on thanks to an extremely rigorous preservation order.

A few steps further on is Retti the candle shop and Schullin the jewellers, both designed by Hans Hollein, and for a long time the only pieces of work in Vienna by this internationally renowned architect. At the corner of Kohlmarkt and Wallnerstrasse it's worth taking a look at the shop belonging to the **Gebrüder Thonet**, who made furniture history with their *Bugholzsessel*, a kind of bent wooden armchair. Anyone who is not already full of Demel cake will enjoy the **Levante**, a few steps down Wallnerstrasse, with its assortment of Levantine vegetable dishes and crunchy döner sandwiches.

A few metres further on turn right into the Haarhof, an old and narrow Viennese street which will take you past the ultra-traditional Esterhazy-Keller and up to the **Naglergasse**. This picturesque street with its fine old burghers' houses – No 13 is particularly attractive – winds its way along what was once the southwestern flank of the Roman garrison of Vindobona.

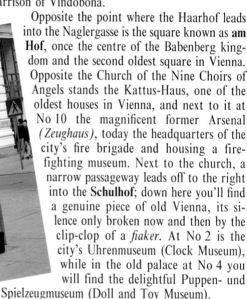

Soloist near the Graben

Opposite the point where the Haarhof leads into the Naglergasse is the square known as **am Hof**, once the centre of the Babenberg kingdom and the second oldest square in Vienna. Opposite the Church of the Nine Choirs of Angels stands the Kattus-Haus, one of the oldest houses in Vienna, and next to it at No 10 the magnificent former Arsenal *(Zeughaus)*, today the headquarters of the city's fire brigade and housing a fire-fighting museum. Next to the church, a narrow passageway leads off to the right into the **Schulhof**; down here you'll find a genuine piece of old Vienna, its silence only broken now and then by the clip-clop of a *fiaker*. At No 2 is the city's Uhrenmuseum (Clock Museum), while in the old palace at No 4 you will find the delightful Puppen- und Spielzeugmuseum (Doll and Toy Museum).

After going left along the Parisergasse you will reach the **Judenplatz**. The most imposing of all the magnificent buildings lining this square is the former **Bohemian Chancellery** at No 11, the work of baroque master builder Johann Bernhard Fischer von Erlach, and today the seat of the Austrian Constitutional Court. Anyone with a sudden craving for Italian *antipasti* can sample the creations at **Da Conte** directly opposite. Those who prefer more substantial Viennese country cooking will enjoy the **Ofenloch** in the adjacent Kurrentgasse.

Next to house No 12 is a passageway leading past a bakery to the horseshoe-shaped **Kleeblattgasse**, which you might earmark for a meal or a night-cap at Kolar or the Seitensprung respectively (both open at 5pm and close at 2am). Both exits of this quiet street lead into the **Tuchlauben**, which leads on the right to the pedestrian zone, specifically the shopping strip of the Graben. Before strolling down this broad avenue, with its mix of expensive stores and popular chains (such as the photo-electronics outlet Niedermeyer), its *Schanigärten* (outdoor pub-gardens) filled to the brim in summer, and its street performers, make sure you see the magnificent figures on the roof of the house at the corner of the Kohlmarkt. The richly ornamented **Trinity Column** in the middle of the street was completed in 1693 at the conclusion of a plague epidemic, hence the name Pestsäule, or Plague Column. No 11, the baroque Bartolotti-Partenfeld Palace also warrants attention for its great verdigris domed roof.

Take a right on the Dorotheergasse for three reasons: a snack of seasoned baguette sandwiches and a Pfiff (beer) at **Tresniewski's**, a cup of coffee with Buchteln (marmalade-filled scones) at Hawelka's opposite, the Viennese coffee-house par excellence, and a visit to the **Jewish Museum** at No 11. After this interlude, go back up the Graben stopping at Habsburgergasse. Looking right you will see the **Peterskirche**, one of Vienna's finest examples of sacred baroque architecture. Going left, you leave the pedestrian zone and reach the **Stallburg**, a Renaissance edifice. Originally built for the Emperor Maximilian, the building was later used as the imperial stables. Today it houses the Lipizzaner horses belonging to the world-famous Spanische Reitschule, or **Spanish Riding School**. The stables are not open to visitors, but performances are held at 10.45am and 7pm on certain days (tickets have to be applied for in writing in advance, though returns/remainders are occasionally available). Training sessions can also be viewed, but again according to a complicated timetable (tickets available from the entrance in the inner courtyard of the Imperial Palace).

Directly opposite the Stallburg and to the right is the Josefsplatz with its baroque **Winter Riding School**, and a little further on, the **Augustinerkirche**, where Emperor Franz Joseph married his beloved Sissy. The latter contains the **Loretto Chapel** with its *Herzgruft* (not to be confused with the Cathedral's *Herzogsgruft*), a vault where the Habsburgs preserved their ancestors' hearts in silver containers.

In the evening head for the **Pfudl** in the Bäckerstrasse, which serves traditional Vienna home cooking such as *Zwiebelrostbraten* (fried beef and onion), or *Beuschel* (calves' heart, lung, liver and sweetbreads thinly sliced and served in a savoury sauce). To round off the day, how about a touch of Viennese elegance – a nightcap in the half-darkness of the **Eden**, the most traditional *Plüschbar* in Vienna? Men must wear a collar and tie.

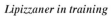
Lipizzaner in training

DAY 3

The Old City

To the Old City between the Schwedenplatz and the Hoher Markt; then along the narrow streets of the Bermuda Triangle to the Jugendstil jewel Ankeruhr (Anchor Clock); Otto Wagner's Post Office Savings Bank. Evening meal in Salzamt.

– U1, U4, tram numbers 1 or 2, or taxi to Schwedenplatz –

The **Schwedenplatz**, on the Donaukanal, borders the oldest section of Vienna. After you emerge from the U-Bahn station exit walk uphill, up the steep steps of the Hafnersteig, to the **Griechengasse**, which takes you straight to a fine example of Old Vienna. Medieval houses stand to the right and left of the thoroughfare, and a rusty sign warns: *Achtung Fuhrwerke* (beware of horse-drawn vehicles). The street narrows to a passageway leading to the **Griechenbeisl** (Greeks' Tavern), once frequented by such famous composers as Beethoven, Schubert and Strauss. It was from the Griechenbeisl – nowadays very touristy – that the famous Pilsner Urquell beer used to be exported around the world. As you head for the historical rooms of this dark wood-panelled tavern, don't be frightened if you suddenly see someone leering through a floor grating: it's the life-sized dummy of **Lieber Augustin**. This legendary Viennese figure once toured the city's streets as a balladeer. He became famous one night when, drunk and singing, he fell down a manhole.

Having passed the Lieber Augustin and three Turkish cannon balls embedded in the wall which were discovered during renovation work in the 1960s, you climb a wooden spiral staircase to a Gothic tower-house: each floor has an idyllic-looking balcony full of lovingly tended plants. Now return to the Griechengasse which leads directly into the **Fleischmarkt**. Almost immediately you will see the magnificent facade of No 13, the **Greek Church**, right next

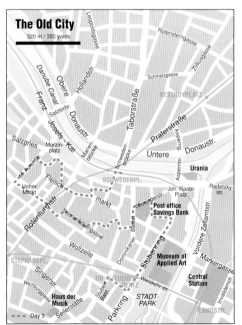

The Old City
320 m / 350 yards

The facade of the Neuer Engel

to the Griechenbeisl; No 15, the **Schwindhof**, built in 1718 and the birthplace of the painter Moritz von Schwind, is also worth a look if the door is open.

From the Griechenbeisl, turn right and make your way past the **Marhold** inn – recommended for anyone keen on hearty Viennese cooking. Only a few steps further on, in the inner courtyard of house No 16, is the enticing **Siddharta** restaurant, the local hero among Vienna's vegetarians.

Continuing towards Rotenturmstrasse, there are fashionable boutiques, the Atelier at No 16, and the elegant arcade belonging to Kapuzina. The right-hand side of the street is dominated by the facades of old shop buildings dating from the 1920s, including the original branch office of the Julius Meinl trading company – in business since 1862. Next to it is the original copper facade of the BAWAG-Haus. At the corner of Rotgasse (beyond Rotenturmstrasse), the stylishly designed **K2** serves the best *sushi* in town. Kiang's next-door is another excellent tip for devotees of Chinese and Thai cuisines. The Kornhäuslturm on Fleischmarkt opposite, is a contrasting Biedermeier tower house, where the author Adalbert Stifter once lived.

Beside it, the Rabensteig takes you down into the middle of the so-called **Bermuda Triangle**. This area between the Rabensteig, Seitenstettengasse and the Ruprechtskirche is where the restaurant boom at the end of the 1970s first took root. The nickname comes from the large number of people who have lost their way touring the restaurants and pubs in the area. At the end of the Rabensteig, at No 5, is the **Neuer Engel**. This pub, considered to be the real heart of the Bermuda Triangle, offers live music every night, along with the beer paradise called **Krah Krah** opposite.

The Seitenstettengasse climbs up left of the Neuer Engel, a street with more bars, and, at No 2, the **synagogue**, built in 1826 by Biedermeier architect Josef Kornhäusl, with its magnificent oval interior; it is the only synagogue to have survived the Nazis' systematic destruction of the area. Taking a right on Judengasse leads to **Ruprechtsplatz**, which is lined with original fashion shops as well as the **Salzamt**, early star of the emerging Vienna restaurant scene in the 1970's, and my recommendation for dinner this evening. Directly opposite the restaurant is the romantically overgrown **Ruprechtskirche**, the oldest church in Vienna.

Now go back to the Judengasse, passing the Arche Noah, a kosher restaurant, and turn right into the **Sterngasse**. The shop on the corner called Firis contains fashions by designers such as Romeo Gigli and Katherine Hamnett; at No 2 you can see the Shakespeare & Company English bookstore, and next door to it is the Finstere Stern, one of the best wine stores in Vienna.

At the end of the Sterngasse a staircase leads down to the Marc-

The Anchor Clock

Aurel-Strasse – to the right is one of Vienna's cosiest cafés, the **Salzgries**. Directly opposite, the old Salvatorgasse takes you to Stoss im Himmel leading to Wipplingerstrasse, where a magnificent **patrician's house**, which was used as the Town Hall until 1885, can be seen at No 8; opposite is the richly decorated rear facade of the former Bohemian Chancellery.

Going down Wipplingerstrasse to the left brings you to the **Hoher Markt**, the oldest market-place in Vienna. Standing in its centre is the **Vermählungsbrunnen** (Marriage Fountain), built by the son of baroque architect Johann Bernhard Fischer von Erlach in 1732. Garda, at No 4, is recommended for fans of ice-cream, and a few metres further on, at No 3, Roman excavations can be visited. Groups of tourists assemble on the hour in front of the **Ankeruhr** (Anchor Clock). This clock, a *Jugendstil* jewel, was completed in 1914 and spans houses 10 and 11 like a bridge. Each

Jesuitengasse

time it strikes the hour it displays a different Viennese historical figure, from the Roman emperor Marcus Aurelius to the composer Joseph Haydn. At noon all 12 figures wander by to musical accompaniment.

At the end of the Hohe Markt you must cross the Rotenturmstrasse again and via the Lugeck enter the 'gateway' to the **Bäckerstrassenviertel** (Bäckerstrasse Quarter), another area popular for its bars. At No 1 Lugeck, gorgeous *belle époque* furniture by Otto Wagner and Joseph Hoffmann can be seen in the the Galerie Ambiente. The Bäckerstrasse forks away to the right, and a colourful relief marks the way to the *Schnitzelkönig* (Schnitzel King) **Figlmüller**, famed for gigantic portions of *Schnitzel*. For the time being, stay on the left side of the street, and stroll down the Sonnenfelsgasse with its immaculately restored old houses; at No 12, steps lead down to the **Zwölf-Apostel Keller** wine bar, much frequented by students, and at No 9 is **Josefine**, the most discreet brothel in Vienna; next to it, **The Bar** attracts scores of night revellers.

Turn left into the small Schönlaterngasse where a passageway at No 5 leads to the magnificent **Heiligenkreuzerhof**. This courtyard is mainly medieval, and a Kunsthandwerksmarkt (craft fair) brings the old walls to life once a month. At the end of the Heiligenkreuzerhof you enter the small Grashofgasse, and via the Köllnerhofgasse return to the Fleischmarkt again. Passing the main Post Office at No 19 (open 24 hours a day), branch off to the left into the narrow Postgasse, and a few metres further on, down the Auwinkel as far as the Dominikanerbastei, where you will see the rear of Otto Wagner's **Post Office Savings Bank**. Passing some elegant burgher houses, go along Wiesingerstrasse, and turn right down Biberstrasse to reach the building's main entrance on the Georg-Coch-Platz.

Built in 1906, the Post Office Savings Bank is one of the main works of *Jugendstil* architect Otto Wagner and with its marble-slab and aluminium facade was the first 'modern' building on the Ringstrasse – a prime example of architecture during the Vienna Secession, which attempted to combine a strict, matter-of-fact approach with decorative flourishes. The spacious hall is distinctive for its elegant functionalism, and it contains some of the original furniture designed by Otto Wagner.

If you are ready for some lunch, adjourn to **Hedrich**, at No 2 Stubenring. This small restaurant, run by top chef Richard Hedrich, is the favourite lunchtime destination of many civil servants from the ministry nearby. Afterwards walk a short way along the Ringstrasse past the Stadtpark to Dr Karl-Lueger-Platz, where you can have coffee in the '50s-style **Café Prückel**.

In the evening return to the Bermuda Triangle for a wander round; for dinner choose between the **Krah Krah**, the **Neuer Engel** or the **Salzamt** restaurants.

Detail of the entrance to the Figlmüller restaurant

1. Parks, Parlament and Palaces

From the Parlament to the Burgtheater, past the elegant palaces on the Freyung to the ancient church of Maria am Gestade.

– U3 to Volkstheater –

The Volksgarten U-Bahn exit leads directly to the park of the same name on the **Ringstrasse**. On the other side of the road is the majestic **Parlament**, built in the 19th century in Greek Revival style.

Enter the Volksgarten from the side that faces the Heldenplatz. Straight away on the right you will see the enticing-looking **Meierei**, a small garden pavilion with a *Schanigarten*, which offers breakfasts in a delightful setting in summer. Between the trees you should be able to make out the columns of the Theseustempel, a favourite meeting-place with the young. A few metres further on there are rows of rose bushes in front of geometrically laid-out flowerbeds. Lots of graceful wrought-iron chairs are lined up here for tired visitors.

Leave the park and head along the Ring for the **Burgtheater**. 'The St Peter's of world theatre' – as this imperial theatre was once described by Rolf Hochhuth – is a mighty round building in Italian Renaissance style. The Viennese like to brag about its commanding role in the German-speaking theatrical world.

Opposite the Burgtheater is the imposing-looking Town Hall (Rathaus). The most distinctive feature of this building, with its neo-Gothic towers, arcades and courtyards, is its 3.4-m (11-ft) high Rathausmann. It's worth taking a brief stroll at this point through the idyllic Rathauspark, with its ancient trees. At Christmas the whole area comes alive with a gaudy market, and in

Monument in front of the Parlament

summer it is a setting for opera-films in cinemascope (daily after sunset, free entrance), when some of the city's finest restaurants set up special stalls here. Then it's time to cross the Ring once again, in the direction of the theatre. To the left of the theatre, a

The Rathausplatz and Burgtheater

stopover at the traditional Café Landtmann is an absolute must. Its spacious rooms and huge terrace are a favourite meeting place for journalists and party functionaries. From here, continue on up the Ring a short way and then turn right down the Schreyvogelgasse. A few steps further on a steep path leads up the Mölkerbastei, part of the city's former fortifications. No 10 is the Dreimäderlhaus, dating from the Biedermeier period. From here there is a good view of the Ringstrasse and the magnificent Alte Universität. The two Gothic spires behind it belong to the tall, sombre Votivkirche, where concerts are regularly held.

Rounding the corner of the Mölkersteig you come to the **Pasqualatihaus** at No 8, one of many places where Beethoven lived. Make a short detour back to the Dreimäderlhaus, then go left through narrow streets over the Mölkersteig and down to the Schottengasse. Directly opposite, a passageway leads from No 2 Helfersdorferstrasse to the Schottenhof: framed by the walls of the monastery that the Babenbergs built in 1155, the shady garden of the **Wienerwald** restaurant is very attractive in the summer. At the end of the Schottenhof, another passageway leads to the Freyung. On the left is the **Schottenkirche**, and opposite is the **Palais Harrach**, which has been crumbling away for years. Haydn's mother was once the family cook there. Opposite the Schottenkirche (Scots' Church) is the magnificent **Palais Kinski**, which you pass on the left in order to go down the Herrengasse.

At No 17 is the shopping arcade of the **Palais Ferstel** – a fine ensemble consisting of brass, glass and marble, crowned by the magnificent **Donaunixen Fountain**. Turn right for a traditional

coffee house, the **Central**. The main entrance is on the corner of Herrengasse and Strauchgasse. If you prefer to have lunch, a good place to choose is the **Bistro** in the middle of the Ferstel-Passage.

At the end of this arcade is the **Freyung**. It was while an underground car park was being constructed below this triangular square in 1987 that sections of the 1156 Babenburg fortress were uncovered.

At the traffic-lights at the end of the Freyung, Tiefer Graben leads off downhill to the left. At No 8 is yet another home of Beethoven. From here you reach the **Hohe Brücke**. The site of the western gate in Roman times, today a magnificent *Jugendstil* stairway leads *zum Glücke* (literally, 'to happiness'), ie up to the Glücksspielstelle (casino) in Wipplingerstrasse. Stay in the Tiefer Graben, however, and go on a little bit further to No 32, with its reddish facade. This is the high-class brothel known as the **Orient Hotel**, which though somewhat tawdry also contains the finest *Plüschbar* in Vienna.

At the end of Tiefer Graben a stairway leads upwards to Am Gestade. One level higher is the majestic 14th-century church of **Maria am Gestade** with its enormously high Gothic windows and a marvellous Gothic helm roof above the entrance. A lot of trendy pubs and bars have sprung up on the square around the church. One of the best is the **Cash** on Schwertstrasse

Inside the Café Central

2. Jugendstil and Markets

Otto Wagner's Jugendstil and the Vienna Secession; a stroll around the Naschmarkt, the Flea Market and the Art and Antiques market by the Donaukanal.

– U1, U2, U4 to Karlsplatz –

The **Otto Wagner Pavilion** stands on the Karlsplatz, a charming memorial to the functional application of Art Nouveau, which was built for the Vienna municipal railway at the turn of the 20th century. For a closer look, take the Resselpark/Karlsplatz exit from the U-Bahn arcade. Then, using the underground passages, find the 'Wiedner Haupstrasse' exit to get to the Kunsthalle, a large yellowish

Pure Jugendstil: The Secession

barracks-like monolith at the west end of the square, which shows changing art and historical exhibitions.

The U-bahn exit marked 'Sezession' leads directly to the temple of Viennese *Jugendstil*, the **Secession Building**. *Krauthappl* ('the cabbage') is the nickname given by the Viennese to the cupola of golden laurel leaves on top of this snow-white exhibition hall, built in 1897. With the foundation of the Vienna Secession, the group of artists that included Gustav Klimt and Otto Wagner became the fathers of Viennese *Jugendstil*. The motto of these rebels is inscribed in sober gold lettering over the entrance: *Der Zeit ihre Kunst, der Kunst ihre Freiheit* (to every age its art, to art its freedom). Klimt's 34-m (111-ft) long **Beethoven Frieze** has been on display downstairs since 1986 – it is a visual interpretation of the composer's Ninth Symphony. The small and colourfully decorated café-bar in the basement is a good place for a short coffee break.

From the Secession Building turn right and cross the Getreidemarkt to the beginning of the Linke Wienzeile and also the **Naschmarkt**, the so-called 'belly of Vienna'. This, Vienna's largest market, was built in 1916 above the Wien River. Mountains of citrus fruit, Arabian spices, Turkish bread and horseflesh are piled high in this 500-m (1,600-ft) long market. Let yourself be carried away – you'll be sure to find all you bargained for and more besides. And on the subject of bargains: the further the stalls are from the city centre, the cheaper they generally are. Don't forget to glance to the right at Otto Wagner's magnificent *Jugendstil* building, the **Majolikahaus**, and its neighbour with the gold-decorated facade by Kolo Moser.

At the end of the Naschmarkt, behind the Otto Wagner station

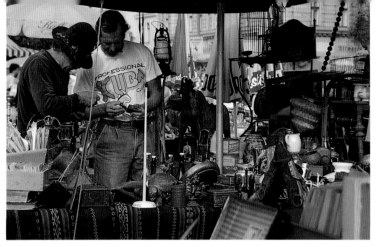

The Saturday flea market behind the station

building in the Kettenbrückengasse a **flea market** is held every Saturday. A talent for hard bargaining combined with luck is essential here, however, if you want to find a nice old antique among the knick-knacks, old clothing and prohibitively expensive lamps doing their best to look *Jugendstil*. The same rules apply here as to flea markets the world over: come in the morning, and keep a close watch on your wallet. You can even begin with breakfast at the **Café Drechsler** in the company of post-disco owls and muscle-bound fruit-and-veg sellers.

At the end of the flea market on the left is the **Brauneis** restaurant (2 Hamburgerstrasse). Those in the know avoid this old-fashioned Viennese tavern on Saturday, preferring to come on Wednesday which is *Schnitzeltag*, Schnitzel-day. At other times, your best bet for lunch is to go back to the Kettenbrückengasse; at No 9 the **Goldene Glocke**, with its fine Viennese cuisine and carefully tended garden, awaits you.

Another open-air market is held at weekends on the Donaukanal, but the **Art and Antiques Market** is a far less professionally run affair – which is actually a very good thing. The best way to get there is to take the U4 at the Kettenbrückengasse in the direction of Heiligenstadt, get out at Schottenring and then turn left before the Salztorbrücke in the direction of the Donaukanal. Improvised open-air stalls offer old books, granny's silver, faded postcards. The food here is rather touristy, but on a fine summer's day it's undeniably pleasant to sip a refreshing drink at the Riverside Bakery or afloat on the *Johann Strauss*.

You may want to save your trip to the Donaukanal market for a Sunday, and perhaps combine it with a short round trip on a boat. Behind the *Jugendstil* Stadtpark station building a magnificent flight of steps leads you down to the Wien river, which at this point is free of flanking buildings. Stroll through the park laid out in memory of the 'waltz king' Johann Strauss. The imposing-looking bronze statue with its marble relief symbolising the Blue Danube waltz is one of the most-photographed sights of Vienna.

3. Window Shopping

From the Opera House, along the Kärntnerstrasse and the Himmelpfortgasse.

– U4, U1 to Karlsplatz, trams 1,2, J as far as the Opera House –

Behind the **Vienna State Opera House**, which is so reminiscent of an Italian Renaissance palazzo, is the start of the city's oldest pedestrian precinct: the **Kärntnerstrasse**. Lined with long-established shops and enlivened by *Schanigärten* (outdoor pub gardens) and street musicians, this stretch of street is ideal for a leisurely stroll.

Begin by making a quick visit to the Vienna **Tourist Information** on Albertinaplatz, where maps of the city and a monthly guide to what's on in Vienna can be collected free of charge seven days a week. A few steps further on, the world-famous *Sachertorte* can be sampled. Before joining the throng of shoppers, the **Malteserkirche** opposite deserves a quick visit.

Now for the shops. At No 41 is the salon belonging to the late doyen of Viennese *haute couture* Fred Adlmüller, where generations of politicians' wives and high-society ladies have bought their ballroom dresses, while at No 13 there's Willi Silbernagel for international men's fashions. Next door to the latter there's elegant porcelain at Wahliss. On the upper floors of Lobmeyer (No 26) there is a glass museum, with fine examples of antique tableware. Anyone who would rather remain in the epoch of Josef Hoffmann and the *Wiener Werkstätte* should then go to Backhausen (on the corner of the Johannesgasse). As well as offering fine fabrics from all over the world, this establishment also specialises in elegant textiles in early 20th-century design. You have to go up to the first floor, though – the ground floor has a ticket-counter and is stuffed with touristy knick-knacks. If you are feeling peckish, visit the Imperial Konditorei (pastry shop) called Heiner at No 21 – its range of delicious cakes is irresistible.

Antique buys

Now stroll a little further along the Kärntnerstrasse and turn right into the attractive Himmelpfortgasse. A few metres further on go left into Rauhensteingasse, to Alexander, a beautifully designed fashion shop. Then return to the Himmelpfortgasse, where at No 6 you will find the oldest coffee house in Vienna, the **Frauenhuber**, which used to be a restaurant owned by the Empress Maria Theresa's personal chef. It's a great place for coffee or lunch. Beside the café is a magnificent baroque burgher's house, its first floor lavishly adorned with angels.

A few steps further on, at No 9, k.u.k. Kuriositäten sells old postcards, badges and mugs painted with the Emperor's portrait. Part of the Finance Ministry resides opposite, at No 8, in Prince Eugene's magnificent Winter palace. Good secondhand clothes and antiques can be found a few steps further on at No 11, Partout, while the Galerie Slavik at No 15 is interesting architecturally. As you walk, look out for the artistically designed shop signs above some of the portals on the left-hand side of the street.

This walk ends where the Himmelpfortgasse reaches the Seiler-stätte, site of the old Ronacher Theatre. On the way back it's worth trying some of the smaller streets that run parallel to the Kärntner-strasse; or you may have worked up an appetite, in which case try the Schwimmende Pyramide, left on Seilerstätte.

Spittelberg

320 m / 350 yards

4. The Spittelberg

A stroll through the Spittelberg, the Biedermeier Quarter, to the smallest home in Vienna.

– U2, U3 or taxi to the Volkstheater –

The Museumsquartier U-Bahn exit leads right to the middle of the baroque ensemble that was built by Johann Bernhard Fischer von Erlach and housed the **Imperial Stables** for 200 years. This magnificent building with its spacious inner courtyards will house a huge museum complex from May 2001.

Cross the Burggasse and stroll past the **Volkstheater** before turning right into Museumsstrasse, where old UFA films are screened at the tiny **Bellaria** cinema. Turn left into the Neustiftgasse, where the traditional inn at No 15, **Anna Rippel**, offers great home cooking. Directly opposite, the small Mechitaristengasse leads to the monastery of the Armenian Mechitarists, hidden behind a plain facade at No 6.

A little further on turn left into Lerchenfelderstrasse. No 13 is one of the finest old *Durchhäuser* (arch-connected houses) in Vienna; a succession of arched courtyards offer a new perspective with each step you take; finally come out into the Neustiftgasse again. Directly opposite, at No 19, the monks' own brand of Benedictine, a liqueur called Mechitarine, is on sale.

A few steps further brings you to the **Ulrichsplatz** on the left, and the little Café Nepomuk. If you go left round the back of the church on the square you will find a row of tiny baroque houses with pretty inner courtyards huddled together; house No 2, built in the

19th century, is particularly delightful. There's a fine rustic pub next door, the **Spatzennest**, with its own very cosy *Schanigarten* (pub garden).

The Burggasse behind the church has unfortunately become the 'motorway' of the 7th District. The fine old portal of the Bäckerei Zöchling on the corner of Burggasse and Sigmundgasse deserves attention, though. Passing some very dusty junk shops, you approach the **Spittelberg**. The Biedermeier house at No 13 is particularly delightful, and a two-floor restaurant here serves traditional Viennese delicacies such as *Rostbraten* (pan-fried sirloin steak) and *Kaiserschöberlsuppe*. Between the 18th and 19th centuries this baroque and Biedermeier quarter was regarded as a sinful red-light district, with one notorious brothel next to another. Saved from collapse in the 1970s, the Spittelberg is a fine example of successful urban renovation.

From the Burggasse you turn right into the Spittelberg's 'high street', the Spittelberggasse, which is closed to cars. The charming house on the corner, Zum Schwarzen Mohren ('the Black Moor'), contains the Bohème pub. As you continue, small galleries, cafés and craft shops greet you almost every step of the way, as do historic plaques on magnificently decorated facades. All of these have a story to relate: house No 22, for example, is called Zum Heiligen Christoph ('St Christopher's) and No 18 Zum Schwarzen Bären (the Black Bear).

People meet here in the little square in front of the splashing fountain for a *crêpe* or one of the healthy but expensive vegetarian dishes served by the **Creperie am Spittelberg**. The monthly *Kunsthandwerksmarkt* (craft fair) here attracts a lot of visitors, as do the many *Schanigärten* in the summer. In December the area hosts one of the best Christmas markets in Vienna. Rents here have become exorbitant for many inhabitants, and the plan to make the area attractive to young artists has never really materialised; nevertheless, visiting this quarter, with its narrow streets and little houses, is a real pleasure for those who enjoy the flavour of the past, and who like to dream of Old Vienna.

Anyone who finds the pubs here too pretentious and expensive would be well advised to go to **Amerlingbeisl** at No 8 Stiftgasse, a street that runs parallel. The inner courtyard of the small baroque house called Zu den drei Herzen (the Three Hearts), overgrown with greenery, serves superb breakfasts and suppers, and the coffee here is excellent.

On the Spittelberg

Now go uphill a little way along the Stiftgasse until you reach the Siebensterngasse. To your right antique shops offer a fine assortment of *Jugendstil* items; to your left, the Siebensterngasse leads down to the Kirchberggasse. Behind the decrepit door at No 16 is an enchanting overgrown garden enclosed by crumbling walls, which leads through to the Siebensterngasse. Opposite, on the corner of Breitegasse and Burggasse, you can admire the smallest house in Vienna: built in 1872 and now a jewellery shop.

Return to the Messepalast via the Burggasse. Opposite are the majestic figures on the roof of the **Naturhistorisches Museum** (Natural History Museum), and to the right, the magnificent dome of the **Kunsthistorisches Museum** (Museum of Fine Arts).

5. Belvedere and the Baroque

A walk from the Karlskirche to the Belvedere via the Schwarzenberg Palace.

– U1, U2, U4 to Karlsplatz –

At the beginning of the 1970s, Alain Delon and Burt Lancaster took part in a breathtaking chase sequence in the film *Scorpio*, filmed in the huge hole made during construction work on the **Karlsplatz** U-Bahn station; today the site lies under the grass of the tiny Ressel Park, disfigured by the bulk of the Kunsthalle.

Only a few steps across the park from the U-Bahn station of the same name is the **Karlskirche**, one of the most important baroque buildings in Europe. This church, built in 1722, with its 72-m (235-ft) high dome and mighty columns looks almost oriental – a sort of mix between St Peter's in Rome and Hagia Sophia in Istanbul.

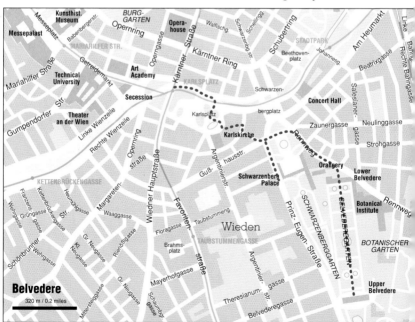

Detail of the Karlskirche

When the Emperor Charles VI laid its foundation stone, the nearby Wien River was still flowing freely. The open space that was meant to be in front of the church has fallen victim to modern town planning, and the small pond with its Henry Moore sculpture is a rather weak apologia. But don't let that spoil your enjoyment of this masterpiece of the baroque.

Leaving the Karlskirche, turn right, passing the **Historisches Museum der Stadt Wien**, until you reach the Schwarzenbergplatz with its fountain, the Hochstrahlbrunnen. If you walk a short way down Prinz-Eugen-Strasse you'll find yourself in front of the entrance to the magnificent **Schwarzenberg Palace**. This masterpiece was the work of baroque architects Lukas von Hildebrandt and Johann Bernhard Fischer von Erlach. From the Palais Restaurant and the Nobel hotel in the right wing of the building there is a superb view of the grand private park.

From here, go back to Schwarzenbergplatz and turn right into Rennweg. At No 6 is the entrance to the park surrounding the **Belvedere**, one of the most magnificent baroque palaces in Europe. In 1714, Prince Eugene of Savoy had a summer palace built in front of the gates of the city, and it is considered the chief and best work of Lukas von Hildebrandt. Right at the Rennweg entrance is the **Lower Belvedere**, which houses the **Baroque Museum**.

From the Lower Belvedere, a walk through a 500-m (1,600-ft) long French garden leads to the **Upper Belvedere**. This summer residence was built in 1721, and was used for official receptions. At the beginning of the 20th century it was the home of the Archduke Franz Ferdinand, the heir to the Austrian throne, whose murder in Sarajevo sparked the beginning of World War I. In 1955 the Austrian State Treaty was signed in the red marble hall here. In the summer *son et lumière* performances in the Belvedere Park illustrate the history of the building. Take a leisurely stroll through the park, and let the harmony of this architectural *Gesamtkunstwerk* sink in. Afterwards you may want to pay a visit to the impressive collection of paintings housed in the Upper Belvedere.

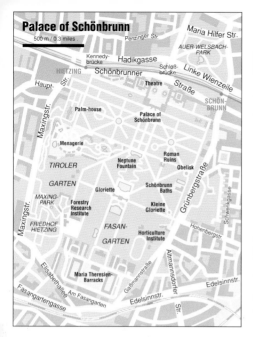

Palace of Schönbrunn

500 m / 0.3 miles

6. Schönbrunn

A stroll through the Schönbrunn Park surrounding the Palace of Schönbrunn; a guided tour of the palace itself, followed by the Gloriette, the Schonbrunner Zoo and the Palm-House.

– U4 to Schönbrunn –

A visit to Vienna wouldn't be complete without a trip to **Schönbrunn**, the summer palace of the imperial family, built by Johann Bernhard Fischer von Erlach. Visitors are obliged to take a guided tour: April to October: daily 8.30am–5pm; November to March: daily 8.30am–4.30pm. Choose a sunny day for your visit and take the U4 as far as Schönbrunn. From there, either walk along the Schlossallee – beware the rather heavy traffic – to the main gate or turn right at the station building and go directly into the **Schlosspark** – a magnificent park complete with topiary and marble statues. If you take the latter option, between April and October it's worth stopping off for a coffee-break at the **Meierei** in the Kronprinzengarten. After that it's not long before you are confronted by the famous yellow facade of the 'Versailles of Austria'. The area here used to be wooded, and it was a glorious spring that gave Schönbrunn its name (*Schöner* = beautiful, *Brunnen* = spring). The Palace was only completed and given its present-day magnificence under Maria Theresa, who resided here for most of her reign.

Within the palace, 45 of the 1,141 rooms are open to visitors. The splendid interior decoration, mostly limited to white and gold, is internationally considered to be one of the greatest achievements of the rococo period.

In the right wing, the **Empress's Ceremonial Apartments**, including the round **Chinese Room**, may be visited. This room, formerly the Empress's study, is nicknamed the Konspirationstafelstube (conspiracy room), for it was used for secret dinners. To avoid untimely interruptions by servants, a fully laid table would simply rise from the middle of the floor.

In stark contrast to all this magnificence are the almost spartan furnishings of the **State Apartments**, where Franz Joseph used to reside. He was born in Schönbrunn in 1830, and died here in 1916. In the left wing are the *salon* of Maria Theresa with its lavish wood panelling, the famous **Vieux-Lacque-Zimmer**, and the **Zere-**

moniensaal. Another famous room is the **Spiegelsaal** (Hall of Mirrors), where Mozart performed at the age of six. It was in the **Blue Chinese Drawing-Room** that Austria's last Emperor, Karl I, signed away his right to rule, and the delegates to the Congress of Vienna once danced in the **Great Gallery**. The Goess apartments off the entrance comprise four rooms with exuberant frescoes by Jan Bergl. If you are interested in old carriages take a look at the **Wagenburg**, a few paces beyond the southwest corner of the courtyard. There are several coachmen's liveries on display, and around five dozen state carriages, including the 4-ton *Imperialwagen*, which was used at coronation ceremonies.

Afterwards, take a short stroll along the wonderful *parterre* as far as the Neptune Fountain. If you continue straight ahead you'll be able to enjoy a magnificent view from the **Gloriette**, a colonnade built in 1775 to round off the southern end of the park (May to October: daily 9am–5pm; coffee house open all year round).

From the Gloriette go slightly left down to the **Schönbrunner Zoo** (May to September: 9am–6.30pm, rest of the year 9am–dusk). This baroque construction was built in 1752, and is the oldest menagerie in the world. One problem though: the modern demands of keeping animals humanely and the facilities provided by old baroque buildings don't always mix.

Schönbrunn

Afterwards, you can look at the **Palmenhaus** (May to September: 9.30am–6pm; October to April: 9.30am–5pm), a fine glass and iron pavilion built in 1880 containing exotic plants.

Now it's time for a well earned rest. Go straight ahead from the Palmenhaus and then left. The route leads out of the Schlosspark on to the Hietzinger Platzl. From here it's only a few minutes to the venerable **Café Dommayer** (Dommayergasse 1). There's a coffee house atmosphere here, combined with all the flair of the *belle époque*, plus a romantic summer-garden.

If you feel like eating something more substantial, the **Hietzinger Bräu** restaurant opposite specialises in 'Old Vienna' meat dishes.

To get back to the city centre again after your meal the best thing to do is to walk back to the Hietzinger Platzl, and then along the edge of the Schlosspark until you reach the nearby U4 station of Hietzing.

Enjoy a walk or cycle ride through the district of Leopoldstadt; visit the Vienna Porcelain Manufactory in the Augarten; the Wurstlprater, the Giant Ferris Wheel that featured in the classic film *The Third Man* **and take a ride on the Lilliput Railway. Afterwards take a stroll in the Prater's woods and meadows; end the day with supper in either the Schweizerhaus or the Lusthaus.**

– U4, U1 to Schwedenplatz –

Vienna's district of **Leopoldstadt** lies on the other side of the Danube Canal. The island formed by the Danube and the canal provides an interesting contrast to the city itself, especially if you don't want to limit your impressions of Vienna to the Opera House and the Hofburg. The best way of discovering Leopoldstadt and the adjoining **Prater** is by bike, which can be rented at the **Salztorbrücke**. Don't be put off by the 'mini-Manhattan' on the north bank of the canal, erected during the 1960s and '70s; in the second postal district beyond, a piece of old Vienna remains intact.

Cross the canal via the **Schwedenbrücke** and continue a little way along **Taborstrasse**. Until the building of the Nordbahn (northern railway) and the regulation of the Danube in 1870, this street was one of the most important in the city. Sandwiched between a row of shops, No 10 is the old **goods exchange**, built in 1890. Fellini was captivated by the atmosphere of the main hall which has housed the **Serapions Theatre** for the last few years. Leopoldstadt, which was formerly the Jewish quarter of Vienna, was always a centre for small businessmen and craftsmen, as well as for industries unwelcome in the city itself, such as abattoirs and tanneries.

Passing the **Spital der Barmherzigen Brüder** (Hospital of the Brothers of Charity) you arrive via the Karmelitergasse at the **Karmelitermarkt**. This is where the Jewish ghetto used to begin. Most of the 60,000 Jews who lived here were deported and murdered during the war. Only their small shops and workshops remain, but the district still exudes its own special atmosphere; definitely Viennese but with a flavour of southeastern Europe. Stroll among the market stalls. Arnold Schönberg and Sigmund Freud both spent their childhood here. The area was once considered of ill-repute; today property prices are rising and Leopoldstadt is on the verge of becoming chic.

Leave the city's former ghetto via the Miesbachgasse and enter the 'feudal' part of district 2, the **Augarten**. Near the entrance to the park on the right stands the **Alte Favorita**, an imperial garden palace, where the young Mozart once played the piano. Today the building houses the **Porzellanmanufaktur Augarten**, the sec-

Idyllic spot in the Prater

ond oldest porcelain manufacturing centre in Europe; the palace just behind it is the home of the Vienna Boys' Choir.

Going along the Heinestrasse, which in former days was lined with tall trees, you leave the Augarten and come to a circular traffic junction known as the Praterstern. From here the Lassallestrasse leads to the Reichsstrasse, to the Danube and the **Mexikoplatz**, where you find the kitschy, pseudo-Romanesque church of St Francis of Assisi.

The Praterstern is also where the **Praterstrasse** ends. The cycle path goes over the Praterstern, past Wien-Nord station and directly to the giant Ferris Wheel. Non-cyclists can take the U1 to Praterstern and continue on to the Lusthaus on a number 80A bus, or 81A, to the Freudenau horse-racing stadium.

People first started riding the 65-m (210-ft) high **Giant Ferris Wheel** in 1897. Along with St Stephen's cathedral, this 500-ton iron construction is a key landmark in Vienna; it also featured in the film *The Third Man*. Around the edge of the actual Prater are the stalls of the **Wurstlprater**. One of the oldest fairgrounds in the world, the Wurstlprater has lost some of its charm through damage suffered in World War II. The magic of the past can only

Ghost train in the Prater

really be reconstructed in the nearby **Prater Museum**, with its posters and photos.

The Viennese atmosphere in the **Schweizerhaus**, on the other hand, is unrelenting. Have a break here: sit under the magnificent horse-chestnut trees, and indulge in the traditional feel of the place; it's at its best if you order a mug of draught Budweiser and a nice grilled *Stelze* (pickled knuckle of pork).

If you would rather keep such substantial fare for the afternoon and have a late breakfast instead, cycle the short distance to No 3 Prater Hauptallee, to the ancient **Café-Meierei-Holzdorfer**. Here you can sit on the terrace surrounded by greenery. The **Prater Hauptallee**, 5km (3 miles) long, leads through magnificent woods and meadows; in 1766 Emperor Joseph II opened this former imperial game reserve to the general public.

At this point you can return to the Wurstlprater and travel 4km (2½ miles) on the **Lilliput Railway** to **Heustadlwasser**, or walk or cycle via the Hauptallee to the **Lusthaus**. This delightful baroque pavilion was once an imperial hunting lodge and a favourite meeting-place for *Herr Barons* and their mistresses. The **Prater grove** is all around you. The only place that should perhaps be avoided at night is around the **Rustenschacherallee** – it's a renowned pick-up area.

8. Coffee Houses

A brief look at a source of much local pride: the famous Viennese coffee house.

Marble-top tables, a small *Brauner* (white coffee) and a glass of water, the daily newspapers and *Herr Ober* (the waiter), elegant as ever with his little bow-tie, who knows exactly how his regular customers like their coffee and has no need to ask. The smell of cigarette smoke, the right atmosphere, and plenty of time – Viennese coffee houses are the perfect antidote to stress.

'In Vienna, people go to coffee houses to get away from it all,' wrote Heimito von Doderer, 'and everyone, an island to himself, sits as far away from everyone else as he can.' Solitude among people of like mind is a very Viennese way of having a good time socially, and is just as much a feature of the modern coffee houses that have sprung up in the city since the 1970s, such as the **Alt Wien**, the **Kleines Café**, the **Salzgries** or the **Hold**, as the more traditional establishments. The leading light of new coffee houses is the **Stein** near the Votiv Kirche, a meeting place for the young and hip who are all so wrapped

The archetypal Kaffeehaus

A welcome awaits

up in themselves that the traditional 'island effect' still survives.

Vienna's first ever coffee house was founded in the 17th century by the Armenian merchant Johannes Diodato. The institution gradually developed into a meeting-place for Vienna's intelligentsia, and eventually became legendary when the *Kaffeehausliteraten* arrived on the scene.

'A *Kaffeehausliterat* is someone in a coffee house who has time to reflect on things that people outside never experience,' Anton Kuh once said about himself and his colleagues. Vienna's coffee house tradition is not the oldest around, but certainly the best cultivated. It even survived the craze for vinyl and Formica that flourished in the prosperous days of the 1950s and '60s. And the restaurant and pub boom of the last two decades has actually given the coffee house a new lease of life – especially those that don't have the appearance of being new, for a Viennese coffee house without any atmosphere is just as appalling a prospect as a *Wiener Schnitzel* without any breadcrumbs.

Establishments that managed to escape the fate of being renovated are: the 1950s-style **Prückel** on the Stubenring; the **Sperl** in the Gumpendorferstrasse, which was opened in 1880 (once the favourite haunt of operetta kings Kálmán and Lehár); and the **Diglas** in the Wollzeile. The modern age has also had very little impact on the **Landtmann**, which is the oldest café on the Ringstrasse.

One of the most attractive as well as one of the oldest of the 500 or so coffee houses in Vienna is the **Frauenhuber** in the Himmelpfortgasse, which once belonged to Maria Theresa's personal chef. Have breakfast here at least once during your visit to the city: breakfast should consists of a roll and butter, a boiled egg, a *Kipferl* (croissant) and a *Melange* (large coffee with lots of milk). Another establishment with a genuinely old coffee house atmosphere is the **Eiles** on Josefstädterstrasse.

The **Central** was once the bastion of the city's *Kaffeehausliteraten*. This 'extended drawing-room' in the Palais Ferstel, formerly filled with poets and philosophers, opened its doors for the first time in decades in 1986 – it's an elegant but, sadly, rather soulless coffee

Café society

house these days. This place, which provided 'refuge for people forced to kill time so as to avoid time killing them' (Alfred Polgar), was frequented at different times by Leon Trotsky, Anton Kuh, Egon Friedell and Peter Altenberg.

The **Griensteidl** on Michaelerplatz, which housed Vienna's *Kaffeehausliteraten* until 1897, was resurrected in 1990 – shiny and bereft of atmosphere. Despite that, it is the only coffee house in Vienna that a bank had to make way for. Sigmund Freud used to play cards here, and Arthur Schnitzler introduced the young Hoffmansthal to the place. When the original Griensteidl was pulled down, Karl Kraus declared: 'The demolition people are turning Vienna into a proper metropolis now'. The interior of the café **Museum** (Friedrichstrasse 6), designed by Adolf Loos in 1899, was also demolished. But this meeting-place for the art world – and a small group of chess-players – has retained its flair, and the paint is stylishly peeling.

In the 1950s, doyen of literature Hans Weigel and H. C. Artmann's Vienna Group transformed the tiny **Hawelka** (Dorotheergasse 12) into *the* meeting-place for avant-garde artists. Wilhelm Holzbauer and Friedrich Torberg used to frequent this coffee house, as did Oscar Werner, Ingeborg Bachmann, Henry Miller and Helmut Qualtinger, to name just a few of its famous patrons. Sadly, its heyday is long gone and most of the clients are now students and tourists, but it's still a popular place to hang out and staff still serve the legendary mini-*Buchteln,* baked yeast dumplings (only after 10pm), along with black coffees and glasses of *Birne* (pear schnapps).

Dummy of Peter Altenberg at one of the tables in the Central

'Heuriger' or new wine is as much a part of Vienna as the waltz or the Big Wheel.

Heuriger is the name given to new wine (*heuer* = this year), usually the product of several types of grape. It is also the name given to the tavern that serves it. The most traditional type of *Heuriger* is the so-called *Buschenschank*, a very simple, rustic tavern either right next to, or even in the middle of, the vineyard that produced the wine.

A bush hanging above the entrance of such a tavern is a sign that *'ausg'steckt is'* (the tavern is open and new wine is available). This custom dates back to 1784 when Emperor Joseph II allowed Vienna's winemakers to serve their own produce. The Viennese were delighted and every Sunday travelled to the suburbs to sit at simple wooden tables under old horse-chestnut trees and sample the new wine accompanied by *Schmalzbrot* (bread and dripping). This pleasant Sunday outing quickly developed into an institution.

Most of the old rustic taverns have now developed into full-blown *Heurigenrestaurants*, though the ones that still serve their own wine can be identified by the magic word *Eigenbau*. The larger establishments have to buy extra wine (their own alone would never suffice) and the sideboards bend under the weight of such substantial delicacies as *Backhendl* (deep fried chicken) and *Schinkenfleckerl* (noodles with diced ham). The famous *Heurigen* village of **Grinzing**, with its Schönbrunn-yellow houses, is inundated by merry hordes of trippers. The legendary Viennese *Weinseligkeit* (literally: 'state of tipsiness induced by wine') is relatively hard to experience here, but if you would still like to get to know Grinzing, go to **Feuerwehr-Wagner** with its magnificent arcaded courtyard (Grinzingerstrasse 53) or to the **Oppolzer**, a higher-class *Heuriger* at Himmelstrasse 22, which offers a fine buffet in the most romantic courtyard in the area, with prices to match.

Ever since the Roman emperor Probus planted vineyards here, Vienna has been the only metropolis in the world to have its own wine. From Bisamberg, north of the Danube, to the slopes of the Kahlenberg, from Mauer in the south to Ober-St-Veit in the west, somewhere in the region of 25,000 hectolitres (550,000 gallons) of wine are produced annually on approximately 700ha (1,730 acres) of land. The former suburbs of Nussdorf, Kahlenberger Dorf, Grinzing, Sievering, Neustift, Stammersdorf and all the rest also play their part in the statistics: the average *per capita* wine consumption here is 35 litres (9 gallons) a year.

Most of the Viennese have their 'own' secret little *Heurigen* where they can indulge in their love of *Weinseligkeit* and *Gemütlichkeit* to the full – the **Baumeister Friedreich** in Ottakring, for example (20 Liebhartstalstrasse), where you can sit on the steep slope of the Wilhelminenberg surrounded by vineyards, and leave the noisy bustle of the city far behind. On the western edge of the city, in Nussdorf or in Kahlenbergerdorf, the atmosphere is almost completely rural – at the **Schübl-Auer** (Kahlenbergstrasse 22) customers sit in a courtyard filled with horse-chestnuts.

There's a highly traditional time to be had north of the Danube, too, in **Stammersdorf**; you can get there on a No 31 tram (from Schottenring/U2). Along the high street you'll find one *Heurigen* after another – with leafy courtyards and simple wooden benches. A large information board at the tram stop will tell you which places have *'ausg'steckt'* (opened their young wine). First though, wander through the alleyways at the foot of the Bisamberg, past the wine-presses and cellars, some of which are 300 years old.

Schrammelmusik is an integral part of the *Heurigen* experience. A type of folk music, it is named after the Schrammel brothers who performed on a concertina and bass guitar at the end of the 19th century. *Heurigen* songs are all about wine, life, death and the transience of things. Most of them are sad, but once you've reached that special state of *Weinseligkeit*, sadness and happiness mingle together. 'Es wird a Wein sein, und wir wer'n nimmer sein' ('Wine will still be around when we're dead').

10. On the Blue Danube

A few minutes from the city centre by U-Bahn you can find surfing, sailing and sun bathing. The following tours can be undertaken on a bicycle or are accessible by public transport.

– U1, Kagran –

Donauinsel

Hire a bicycle at the Danube Canal near Salztorbrücke and follow the signposted cycle path to the **Reichsbrücke**, from where you can drive onto the 21-km (13-mile) long artificial island (the Donauinsel), which was built in 1981. There is a station near the bridge (U1-Donauinsel).

The **Donauinsel** is a byproduct of the construction of the New Danube canal, which was equipped with sluice gates and designed to counter flood-

Summer pursuits

ing. A 200-metre (600-ft) wide strip of land between the new canal and the old river, the island has since become a recreational resort with Austria's longest beach (40 km/24 miles) and long paths for pedestrians and bicycles. Only a few minutes from the city centre, it is ideal for jogging, cycling, surfing, sailing, swimming, rowing and skateboarding.

Leisure facilities begin at the Reichsbrücke at the **Copa Kagrana**. Here, about 40 bars and restaurants – including Turkish, Greek and Italian – try to create a seaside holiday atmosphere in the heart of Vienna. Open-air discos thrive at night. The **Donauinselfest**, a spectacular festival with concerts, cabaret and theatre performances, is held here every June.

North of the Copa is the **Aquadrom**, Austria's longest water chute, and next to it the **Aquadrom Beach Club** with its disco and barbecue. The northern part of the island is usually less busy: here, you can swim in small, sandy bays while enjoying a view of the hills of the Vienna Woods. Sailors find the best conditions for their sport around this part of the island.

Trams 31 and 32 will drop you at the northern end of the island. In the southern half, opposite the left bank of the New Danube canal between Wehr (weir) 2 and Lobgrundstrasse, nudists will find their own patch of paradise. And if you want to dine *al fresco* with your friends, you can book one of the many barbecue areas (tel: 4000, direct line 82 677).

The Old Danube

Continuing along the cycle path from the Reichsbrücke, you come to the **Old Danube**, a former branch of the Danube river. Here you will find plenty of unofficial spots to swim as well as public bathing areas such as the **Gänsehäufl** (which literally and unfortunately translates as 'goose droppings'). The Gänsehäufl can also be reached by underground (U1 to Kagran) or by bus (91A to the terminus). A foot-bridge crosses over to the island. The Gänsehäufl is one of the oldest public baths in Europe, dating from the turn of the 20th century.

Further north are the **Strandbad Alte Donau** and the **Arbeiterstrandbad** (workers' baths). Both can be reached on the U1 (Alte Donau). From there you have to take the bus (20B) or walk along An der Oberen Alten Donau. They offer further opportunities for recreation, from simply lying on the river bank to hiring a boat for sailing, or paddling a pedalo.

There are numerous delightful garden bars and restaurants in this area. Ones to try include **Birners Strandgasthaus** (An der Oberen Alten Donau 47) or the **Neubrasilien** (An der Unteren Alten Donau 61).

11. Museums

A selection of the best collections in Vienna's museums.

– U2/U3 to Volkstheater –

It would be a shame to visit Vienna without looking at its museums. The magnificent, domed **Kunsthistorisches Museum** (Museum of Fine Arts, Maria Theresienplatz) for example, is one of the most important art museums in the world, and contains masterpieces by Breughel, Tintoretto, Titian and Rubens.

The **Naturhistorisches Museum** (Museum of Natural History) is in the twin building opposite. Exhibits include the oldest collection of meteorites in the world, the largest opal ever found in Europe and a palaeontological collection.

Vienna also has the largest collection of graphic art in the world. The **Albertina** (Augustinerstrasse 1), contains 1.9 million examples of printed graphic art and drawings spanning five centuries – from Michelangelo and Dürer to Raphael, Rembrandt and Picasso. Anyone interested in 19th- and 20th-century art will find a remarkable collection of masterpieces by Klimt and Schiele, Kokoschka, Boeckl and Wotruba in the **Österreichische Galerie** (Austrian Gallery) in the Upper Belvedere.

A few minutes away from the Belvedere is the **Museum des 20 Jahrhunderts** (Museum of the 20th Century). The former Austria pavilion of the Brussels World Fair of 1958 features various exhibitions taken from the **Museum Moderner Kunst** (Museum of Modern Art), which has been in the Palais Liechtenstein since 1979. Exhibitions of contemporary art can also be seen at the **Kunsthalle** on Karlsplatz, at the **Kunstforum** (Freyung 8) and at the **Kunst-HausWein** (1030 Untere Weissgerberstraase 13).

Vienna's **Museum für Angewandte Kunst** (MAK; Museum of Applied and Decorative Art, Stubenring 5) is the oldest of its kind in Europe. Exhibits include furniture, carpets, porcelain and textiles from the Middle Ages to the present day. At the Hofburg is the **Schatzkammer** (Imperial Treasury, with the 1,000-year-old Imperial Crown).

The **Historisches Museum** (Historical Museum, Karlsplatz) documents Vienna's history from the Stone Age to the present day; highlights here include scale models of the city's development, stained glass from the Cathedral and Adolf Loos' drawing-room.

A new attraction for music lovers is the **Haus der Musik**, full of state-of-the-art interactive installations and historical information, especially about Viennese composers. Adjacent is a museum dedicated to the world-famous Vienna Philharmonic Orchestra.

Vienna has a large number of small museums – **Theatermuseum** in the Lobkowitz palace, **Uhrenmuseum** (Horological Museum, Schulhof 2), **Sigmund Freud Museum**, in Freud's former home at Berggasse 19, **Beethoven Museum** (Probusgasse 6), **Mozart Museum** (Figarohaus, Domgasse 5) and **Haydn Museum** (Haydngasse 19), to name but a few.

12. Splendid Cemeteries

A walk through some of Vienna's finest burial grounds.

–Tram No 71, from Schwarzenbergplatz –

The relationship of the Viennese people to death is legendary. They spend their lives saving money at a *Sterbeverein* ('death club') in order to be a *'schöne Leich'* ('a nice corpse') and be given an elegant and fitting *Pompfüneberer* (funeral) accompanied by the sound of wailing violins. Most Viennese songs are also preoccupied with death – a mixture of acceptance of fate and a strong yearning:*'Verkauft's mei G'wand, i fahr in Himmel'* ('I'm off to Heaven – sell my clothes').

Every year on All Saints' Day the city's tram system provides 500 extra carriages on route 71 to convey nearly a million people to the **Zentralfriedhof** (central cemetery) in Simmering, which lies alongside Vienna's longest street, the Simmeringer Hauptstrasse. Before the airport *Autobahn* was built, the first sight most visitors had of Vienna was of the infinitely long wall of this cemetery, the largest in Austria, whose 2 million graves outnumber the actual population of the city.

The Zentralfriedhof

Get off No 71 tram at Friedhofstor 1. Behind it is the **Jewish Cemetery** – an overgrown wilderness, with a few of the tombstones still lying on the ground. Thanks to a major volunteer effort the cemetery has been tidied up. Many relatives of the dead who lie here were deported and murdered. The graves are divided into groups, and in group 5b Arthur Schnitzler, Friedrich Torberg and Karl Kraus lie buried. Also here is the grave of Gustav Pick, long-forgotten composer of the famous *Fiaker Song*.

Along the cemetery wall, the route leads to the main gate of the Zentralfriedhof, **Tor (Gate) 2**, built by Max Hegele, who in 1905 also constructed the imposing **Dr Karl-Lueger-Remembrance Church**, a short distance to the left of the main gate. This church, with its vast dome, is considered a *Jugendstil* masterpiece. Instead of numerals, the clock-face spells out the letters *Tempus Fugit* (Time Flies).

To the right and left of the main path is probably the largest collection of 'tombs of honour' in the world. Approximately 1,000 personalities lie buried in this cemetery, which was opened in 1874. Every day, huddles of camera-clicking Japanese stand in front of

Schubert's tomb

the graves of Beethoven, Brahms, Mahler and Schubert.

The silhouette of a bat can be made out on the gravestone of waltz king Johann Strauss the Younger, a tribute to what is probably his most famous opera, *die Fledermaus*; the grave of comedian Helmut Qualtinger is adorned with a sculpture by Alfred Hrdlicka, and actor Curt Jürgens was the first to receive a nocturnal burial at his own request. His tombstone is jet black marble. Mozart has been given a monument in group 32a, but he was actually buried in a mass grave for the day's dead at St Marx's Cemetery *(see below)*.

The cemetery, with its 15,000 trees, is one of the largest expanses of green in the city, and its surface area – 2.4 sq km (1 square mile) – is nearly as large as Vienna's District 1. It even has its own hunting association to take care of the many rabbits, pheasants and partridges that inhabit the area.

The 300,000 graves offer a fascinating record of Viennese social history – there are splendid vaults, paupers' graves, and the names of Italian, Serbian and Hungarian noblemen and captains in the imperial cavalry. The cemetery has its own bus, and a plan detailing the grave numbers can be obtained from the supervisor at the main gate. Around All Saints' Day, flower sellers, sausage stalls and *Maronibrater* (hot chestnut vendors) spring up around the gate, ready for business.

Opposite the main gate is the majestic-looking **crematorium**, built by Clemens Holzmeister in 1922. This Byzantine-Expressionist building is enclosed in the walls of the Renaissance palace of **Neugebäude**, a summer residence of the emperor Maximilian dating from the 16th century that fell into disrepair soon after its completion. A substantial amount of its splendid façade decoration was used in the construction of the Gloriette at Schönbrunn. During the Turkish siege of 1529 – which didn't succeed, but did bring coffee to Vienna – the Sultan's tent is rumoured to have stood here. If you cross the allotments, it's possible to walk along the walls of the palace's former pheasantry.

The enticing-looking **Schloss Concordia** is situated opposite gate No 1 of the cemetery. This romantic pavilion, restored in 1988, in the middle of its sleepy garden, is a cross between a café, a restaurant and a literary salon. The interior is crowned by a *Jugendstil* glass roof. If you have the time and the appetite for more graves, take a No 71 tram back towards the city centre until you reach the magnificent **St Marx's Cemetery** at Leberstrasse 6. It has been deconsecrated for over 100 years and is Vienna's last *Biedermeier* cemetery. Today it is a romantic park, filled in spring with the

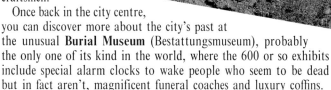

View of the Kahlenberg

heady scent of lilac blossom. It was here, in 1791, that Mozart was buried, in an unmarked grave. Walk a short way through this restful place, past the graves of silk manufacturers and small-time craftsmen.

Once back in the city centre, you can discover more about the city's past at the unusual **Burial Museum** (Bestattungsmuseum), probably the only one of its kind in the world, where the 600 or so exhibits include special alarm clocks to wake people who seem to be dead but in fact aren't, magnificent funeral coaches and luxury coffins.

Still on this macabre note, you may want to go on to the **Josephinum**, founded in 1785 by Joseph II as a Military Academy of Surgery and Medicine.

13. Tales from the Vienna Woods

Three walks through the Vienna Woods.

When the Viennese fancy a walk in the woods, they don't have far to travel. The **Vienna Woods** *(Wienerwald)*, the 50-km (30-mile) long northeastern foothills of the Alps extend into the city itself.

In the Danube area they drop steeply and surround the city rather like an amphitheatre. Dense mixed forest, gentle hills and slopes with vineyards and small *Heurigendörfer* (wine-producing villages) are inviting destinations. In the summer the ground underfoot is covered with thick moss; in spring the air is full of the scent of wild garlic; and in autumn colourful leaves rustle beneath your feet. It is a magnificent recreation area, with slender elms, majestic beech trees and mighty oaks. Proximity to the city has its disadvantages, however: it is estimated that some 60 percent of the trees here are affected by pollution.

You can go by car to the Vienna Woods, or by public transport – or even on foot. If possible avoid weekends, when the marked routes and restaurants are jammed with Viennese on day-trips.

Kahlenberg and Leopoldsberg

Take the U4 as far as **Heiligenstadt** and then bus number 38A. This takes you up to the Cobenzl, the Leopoldsberg and the Kahlenberg via the wine village of Grinzing and the **Höhenstrasse**. If travelling by car you can drive the entire length of the Höhenstrasse as far as Hütteldorf, or you can branch off at Kahlenberg and go to Klosterneuburg. The old, open-air Krapfenwaldl swimming pool is a favourite in summer and a great place for a bird's-eye view of the city.

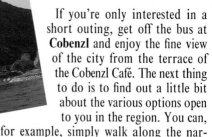

If you're only interested in a short outing, get off the bus at **Cobenzl** and enjoy the fine view of the city from the terrace of the Cobenzl Café. The next thing to do is to find out a little bit about the various options open to you in the region. You can, for example, simply walk along the narrow Reisenbergweg past some vineyards and down to **Grinzing**, where you can catch the bus again. If you want a longer ramble, walk a little further along the Höhenstrasse from Cobenzl, and then turn left down Himmelstrasse. If you then follow the sign saying *zur Bellevuestrasse* you'll come to a small monument. This is the former site of the 'Belle Vue' villa, where Sigmund Freud came to spend his summers. Now take the Himmelstrasse back again, where at No 22 the Oppolzer – one of Vienna's most romantic (and expensive) *Heuriger* – awaits you. Afterwards you can take a walk through the **Gspöttgraben** to the neighbouring village of **Sievering**. There are some wonderful *Heurigengärten* here, too. Bus No 39A will take you back to the U-Bahn at Heiligenstadt.

You can travel on from Cobenzl with a No 38A bus, and discover the **Kahlenberg** and the **Leopoldsberg** hills. The **Festungsturm** (fortified tower) of a fortress once built by the Babenbergs up on the Leopoldsberg affords a magnificent view of the Danube and the city. The **Sobieski Chapel** is a reminder of the time when the King of Poland rushed to assist the Viennese in their fight against the Turks. Both mountains have restaurants to greet weary wanderers. Here you can put your feet up, have something to eat and, above all, enjoy the superb views.

Up the Hermannskogel

An excursion to the legendary mountain known as the **Hermannskogel** is also worthwhile and not too strenuous. To get there, from Heiligenstadt (U4) take a 39A bus all the way to its terminus in **Sievering**. Here, go uphill along the Agnesgasse and then turn right on to the Salmannsdorfer Höhe when you come to the wayside shrine.

Go under the Höhenstrasse and then turn left, following the red markers, until you reach the 454-metre (1,480-ft) high **Dreimarkstein** mountain with its fine view. You can go into the little **Häuserl am Roan** restaurant, then go back downhill to the right, following the blue markers this time, which take you past the **Grüaß-di-a-Gott** restaurant on the Rohrerweise to Hermannskogelweg. If you now follow the green markers you'll soon reach the top of the **Hermannskogel**. From the Habsburgwarte observation point, built in 1888, you will be greeted by a magnificent view; visibility here on clear days is over 180km (110 miles), all the way to the Traunstein in the west.

Calendar of Special Events

gins on the 11th day of the 11th month, ie 11 November, but on that day in Vienna you'll be more likely to be invited to a *Martinigansl-Essen*, where people dine on roast goose in honour of St Martin.

The season of the great balls and *Gschnase* (fancy dress balls) only begins in earnest once the New Year has started. The ball starts rolling, so to speak, with the *Kaiserball* (Imperial Ball) in the Hofburg, and the real highlight is the dazzling *Opernball* (Opera Ball), attended by the Austrian President, on the last Thursday of the Carnival season. Almost every professional association and club holds its own special ball, including the police force, café-owners, chimney-sweeps, hunters (wearing traditional green) and also doctors, lawyers, pharmacists and firemen. At the *Zuckerbäckerball* (sweetmakers' ball) a Ball Queen is selected, and her weight in sweets is donated to children's homes.

Debutantes throng to the Opernball and the Philharmonikerball as well as to Rudolfina Redoutee. The official *Ballkalender* (Ball Calendar) appears in the late autumn and may be

JANUARY / FEBRUARY

New Year's Eve (Silvester): The Viennese assemble on the Stephansplatz to see in the New Year when the big bell called the *Pummerin* strikes 12; in the Musikverein the Vienna Philharmonic perform their New Year's Concert *(Silvesterkonzert)* which is broadcast worldwide; the Imperial Ball *(Kaiserball)* is held in the Hofburg.

Fasching (Carnival) and Ball season: *Fasching*, or Carnival, officially be-

obtained from the Stadtinformation (information office) at the Town Hall, Friedrich-Schmidt-Platz 1, 1082 Wien.
Ash Wednesday (Aschermittwoch): At the end of Carnival, most restaurants and hotels 'sweeten' the transition to the dreariness of Lent with a huge *Heringschmaus* (herring banquet).

MARCH / APRIL

Vienna Spring Fair (Wiener Frühjahrsmesse): In March, the traditional Vienna Spring Fair is held on the exhibition site in the Prater.
Fashion Fair (Modemesse): In April and October the avant-garde fashion fair Off-Line moves into the Hofburg.
City Festival (Stadtfest): On the last Saturday in April, the traditional City Festival sponsored by the ÖVP (the conservative Austrian People's Party) livens up Vienna's streets and squares with an assorted programme of music, cabaret and theatre.
Osterklang (Sound of Easter): the music festival of the Vienna Philharmonic.

MAY / JUNE

Spring Marathon (Frühlingsmarathon): During the second half of May, Vienna greets the spring with a large-scale city marathon.
Vienna Festival (Wiener Festwochen): In May and June this arts festival, both traditional and avant-garde, takes place at venues all over Vienna.
Danube Island Festival (Donauinselfest): This is the SPÖ's (Social Democrats) answer to the City Festival; it takes place on the Donauinsel on the last weekend of June.

JULY / AUGUST

Vienna Musical Summer (Wiener Musiksommer): A very wide ranging programme of musical performances held in a variety of attractive venues, from the Staatsoper (State Opera House) and the Arkadenhof (Concert Courtyard) in the Town Hall to churches and old palaces.
Dance Festival Im-Puls (Tanz-Wochen): Every two years (even years: 1998, 2000, 2002, etc), in July/ August, Vienna hosts a large Dance Festival.
Vienna Jazz Festival: taking place in various clubs around the city and in the State Opera.

SEPTEMBER / OCTOBER

Vienna Autumn Fair (Wiener Herbstmesse): The Vienna Autumn Fair begins in September.
National Holiday (Nationalfeiertag), 26 October: Recently declared National Hiking Day. Entry to Vienna's museums is free on this day.
Modern Vienna (Wien Modern): This festival of contemporary music is held between the end of October and the end of November in Musikverein and Kouterthaus.

DECEMBER

Christmas Markets (Christkindl märkte): Christmas markets take place on December weekends on the Spittelberg and on the Freyung. There' also an art market in the Heiligenkreuzerhof, and the square in front of the Town Hall is the venue for th Vienna Christmas Market *(Wiener Christkindlmarkt)* – see also 'Markets' in the *Shopping* chapter, page 66.

Further information about special events and festivals taking place in Vienna can be obtained from Vienna Tourist Information (Albertinaplatz) from Stadtinformation (Town Hall Friedrich-Schmidt-Platz 1, 1082 Wien and also in the *Falter* and *City*, th two weekly *What's On* guides.

Shopping

The following list of shops is a personal selection of long established favourites and new discoveries, and all of them should offer plenty of ideas to tempt you to part with your *schillings* in Vienna.

Books and Magazines

Whether it's a travel guide you're after, a map or a hiking guide – **Freytag & Berndt** (Kohlmarkt 9) will almost certainly have it in stock. The **Morawa** bookshop (Wollzeile 11) is well laid-out and stocks domestic and international newspapers. International books and magazines on art and architecture can all be found at the **Prachner** bookshop (Kärntnerstrasse 30) and the **Wolfrum** (Augustinerstrasse 10); those looking for large and expensive art books will appreciate the **Sallmayer'sche Buchhandlung** (Neuer Markt 6). The **Gerold** bookstore (Graben 31) and **Frick** (Graben 27) offer a wide selection of national and international books, as does the **Zentralbuchhandlung** (Schulerstrasse 1–3). Books and magazines in English can be found at **Shakespeare & Company** (Sterngasse 2) and in the **British Book Shop** (Weihburggasse 8); French books are at **Bateau Livre** (1090, Liechtensteinstrasse 37). The widest range of feminist literature and social science publications is found at the **Frauenbuchhandlung** (1080, Langegasse 11). Anyone interested in political science should drop in at **Heinz Kolisch** (Rathausstrasse 18). Unusual and esoteric books are waiting to be discovered at **777** (Domgasse 8) and **Südwind** (1030, Baumgasse 79); the best though is **OM Esoterik** (1090 Althanstrasse 33). A real treasure trove is **Hintermayer** (1070, Neubaugasse 29 and 1060, Gumpendorferstrasse 51), which sells remaindered books at unbelievably low prices.

Most of the newspaper kiosks in the city centre are open seven days a week and usually stock a good selection of international as well as domestic papers and magazines.

Laid-back lines

Austriana and Antiques

Few cities have such a plethora of antique shops in such a small area as Vienna; they are all clustered around the **Dorotheum**. *Tante Dorothee* or *Pfandl* are just two of the nicknames for the oldest auction house in Europe. It was founded as a pawnbroker's in 1788. For over 200 years now the Dorotheum has occupied a former monastery in the Dorotheergasse (Dorotheergasse 11 and 17).

The largest selection of imperial Austrian knick-knacks is found at **k.u.k. Kuriositäten** *(*Himmelpfortgasse 9). **Duschek & Scheed** (Plankengasse 6) specialise in old watches; paintings and *objets d'art* can be found at **Reinhold Hofstätter** (Bräunerstrasse 12), *Jugendstil* objects at **Zetter** (Lobkowitzplatz 1), antique glass at **Kovacek** (Spiegelgasse 12), wonderful furniture and glass at **Monika Kaesser** (Krugerstrasse 17), and antique sheet music at **Doblinger** (Dorotheergasse 10).

Markets

Halfway between expensive antiques on offer from professional dealers and cheap junk, you just might (if you have patience as well as luck) find the odd fine piece at the Vienna flea market, or **Flohmarkt** (every Saturday until 6pm; U4/Kettenbrückengasse). Anyone who enjoys browsing around market stalls should also visit the **Naschmarkt**, Vienna's largest daily market, between the Karlsplatz and Kettenbrückengasse.

From May until September the **Kunst und Antiquitätenmarkt** (Arts and Antiques market) is held at the Donaukanal (Saturday 2–8pm, Sunday 10am–8pm; U2/Schottenring).

On the Spittelberg in district 7, a **Kunsthandwerksmarkt** (Arts and Crafts Fair) is held for four weeks during the Christmas season (U2, U3 Volkstheater); in the Heiligenkreuzerhof a **Kunstmarkt** (Art Market) is held on the first weekend in every month.

Arts, Crafts and Textiles

Whether it's English velvet, French silk or material with *Wiener Werkstätte* (Vienna workshops) designs all over it – **Backhausen** (Kärntnerstrasse/Johannesgasse) has absolutely everything. Gorgeously coloured fabrics are also stocked at **India** (Strobelgasse 2).

Arts and crafts from Österreichische Werkstätte are found at Kärntnerstrasse 6, and quite a few charming and original pieces can be found at the Arts and Crafts Fair at the Spittelberg *(see under Markets)*.

Prints, Posters and Postcards

The best place for elegant prints by old and new masters is **Wolfrum** at Augustinerstrasse 10; the **Galerie Image** (Ruprechtsplatz 4–5) has a large selection of posters with frames and also some very fine postcards; original postcards can also be obtained at the **Karteninsel** (1140, Ernst Bergmanngasse 10).

CDs and Tapes

EMI **Austria** (Kärntnerstrasse 30) has a good selection covering all genres; for a specialist classical music shop try **Ascolta** (Kärntnerstrasse 59). A large selection of pop, jazz, rock and oldies are on offer at **Black Market** (Gonzagagasse 9); jazz fans should take a look at **Red Octopus** (1080, Josefstädterstrasse 99) and **Teuchtler** (1060 Windmühlgasse 10); and it's hard to leave the CD shop **Havlicek** (Herrengasse 5) without a couple of new discs under your arm. **Virgin Megastore** has opened an outlet on the Mariahilferstrasse (Nos 37–39)

Glass, Porcelain and Tableware

Anyone keen on elegant tableware will love **Lobmeyr** (Kärntnerstrasse 26); glass design there ranges from Josef Hoffmann to Matteo Thun. If you're keen to buy, make sure you also take a look at **Bakalowits** (Spiegelgasse 3).

The products of the former imperial porcelain manufacturers **Augarten** can be bought at the corner of Graben and Seilergasse, and a few doors down is **Rasper** (corner of Graben and Habsburgergasse).

Distinctive designs

People after unusual tableware should visit **Ostovits** (Stephansplatz/Jasomirgottstrasse). For elegant knives and forks, **Berndorf** (Wollzeile 12) is good, as are **Besteck-Kistl** (Lichtensteg/Bauernmarkt), WMF (Stock-im-Eisen-Platz 3) or the very exclusive **Christofle** (Jasomirgottstrasse 3–5).

Jewellery

Graben and the Kohlmarkt are where the city's long established jewellery firms are based, some of which still proudly use the old imperial prefix *k.u.k. Hoflieferant*. **Kiss & Rozsa** (Kohlmarkt 16) do fine silver jewellery. A few steps further on, **Schullin** (Kohlmarkt 7) not only has exclusive jewellery, but also has a magnificent portal by top architect Hans Hollein. In the Graben we have **Haban** (Graben 12 and Kärntnerstrasse 2) and **Heldwein** (Graben 13). Particularly fine silver jewellery can be seen at **Kecksilber** (Trattnerhof and Bäckerstrasse 10). **Galerie V&V** (Bauernmarkt 19) specialises in modern designer jewellery from Austria and abroad, and **Schmollgruber** can be found in the smallest house in Vienna (1070, Burggasse 27).

Knick-knacks, Presents & Souvenirs

Karfunkel (Morzinplatz 4) sells all manner of wacky presents and fashion jewellery; **Paperbox** (Stephansplatz 6 and Graben 29A) offers small gifts and souvenirs; **Waltz** (Kärntnerstrasse 46) offers accessories of all sorts. Gifts and crazy stationery can be found at **Funkart** (1060 Mariahilferstrasse 77–79); **Eva Eder** (1080, Langegasse 19) offers attractive and unusual glassware. There's a large selection of candles at a shop called **Retti** designed by Hans Hollein (Kohlmarkt 10); all kinds of souvenirs are provided by **Hannerl** (Jasomirgottstrasse 4). Exclusive items can be found at **Theyer & Hardtmuth,** (Kärntnerstrasse 9), specialists in exclusive writing utensils. **Haas & Haas** (Stephansplatz 4, is good for specialist teas, small presents and souvenirs.

Spectacles

Most of the international names in designer spectacles are manufactured in Austria. Try **Hartmann** (Singerstrasse 8/entry to Liliengasse); **Schau Schau** (Rotenturmstrasse 11/Ertlgasse); and **Optiker Maurer** (1080, Josefstädterstrasse/Buchfeldgasse).

Design and Furniture

Italian and Scandinavian furniture and beautiful designer furniture can be found at **Wolfgang Bischof** (Judenplatz 6), **Passini** (Franziskanerplatz 6), **Henn** (Naglergasse 29), **Silenzio** (Salzgries 2), **Prodomo** (1150, Flachgasse 35), **Go-In** (1070 Mariahilferstrasse 20), **Hartmann Henn** (Naglergasse 29) and also at **Accento Nuovo** (1090, Kinderspitalgasse 1).

Furniture by designers such as Josef Hoffmann, Otto Wagner and Kolo Moser can be bought for a small fortune at the **Galerie Ambiente** (Lugeck 1) and at **Monika Kaesser** (Krugerstrasse 17). Anyone looking for an authentic *Jugendstil* piece should walk down the Siebensterngasse behind the Spittelberg in district 7, where several well equipped shops can be found. Fans of antique furnishings are also recommended to pay a visit to **F.O. Schmidt** (1090 Währingerstrasse 28).

Shoes for sale

Linen & Lingerie

The **Schwäbische Jungfrau** (Graben 26) does fine tablecloths and bed-linen, as does **Gans** (Brandstätte 1). Silk lingerie can be found at **Rositta** (Kärntnerstrasse 17); it's also worth visiting **La Biancheria** (1080, Josefstädterstrasse 27), **Per la Donna** (Judenplatz 5) and **Wolford** (Wollzeile 37).

Shoes & Leather Goods

People looking for something special are advised to go to **Tardi's** (Kärntnerstrasse 37, Bauernmarkt 2 and Graben 17), **d'Ambrosio** (Jasomirgottstrasse 4–6 and Bauernmarkt), **Zak** (Kärntnerstrasse 36) and **Dominici** (Singerstrasse 2). For designer shoes, try **Denkstein** (Bauernmarkt 8). Made-to-measure shoes are manufactured by **Rudulf Scheer** (Bräunerstrasse 4).

As far as leather is concerned, **Bottega Veneta** is excellent but very expensive (Stock-im-Eisen-Platz 3/entrance to Seilergasse); handmade bags and accessories are the specialities of **Horn** (Bräunerstrasse 7); highly exclusive leather goods can be purchased at **Louis Vuitton** (Kohlmarkt 16); and high-quality hand-made goods can be found at **Franz Schulz** (Führichgasse 6). The **Kofferzentrale** (1060, Mariahilferstrasse 3) offers suitcases and handbags in every conceivable shape, size and colour.

Elegant Fashion & Haute Couture

British chic and modern fashion is found at **Kowalski**, **Piccina** and **Mac's** in the Brandstätte; international names in haute couture can be found at **Jonak** (Trattnerhof), **Trussardi** (Tuchlauben 11 and the Haas-Haus on the Stephansplatz), **Jil Sander** (Bauernmarkt) and

Sign language

Sonia Rykiel (Goldschmiedgasse 5). **Etoile** (Lugeck/Köllnerhofgasse) and **Cellini** (Jasomirgottstrasse 5) both stock Armani, Krizia and Valentino. Conservative British style is worshipped at **Ita** and **Braun** at Graben 8 and 18 respectively. **Popp & Kretschmer** (Kärntnerstrasse/Walfischgasse) and **Adlmüller** (Kärntnerstrasse 41) specialise in super-elegant dresses.

Men's Fashion

The men's fashion specialists in Vienna are **Willi Silbernagl** (Kärntnerstrasse 13–15), **Guys and Dolls** (Schultergasse 2) and **Sir Anthony** (Kärntnerstrasse 21); **fil à fil** (Brandstätte 7–9) has a huge assortment of men's shirts; tailor-made clothing can be obtained from the best tailor in the city, **Knize** (Graben 13).

Young People's Fashion

The creations of **Helmut Lang**, an Austrian fashion designer who has had great success both in Paris and New York, can be found at

Window on fashion

Seilergasse 6. **Schella Kann** is the place to go for a fresh angle on classics (Singerstrasse 6/2/8 and Seilergasse 3); **Mango** (Kärntnerstrasse 22) is the place for elegant understatement; and Austrian knitted designs, classical and original, are found at **Haider-Petkov** (Kohlmarkt 11); and **Annette Beaufays** (Bäckerstrasse 10) offers young avant-garde style.

Classic fashion is also found at **Cachil** (Ringstrassengalerien) and at **Giarratana** on the Lugeck; relaxed young elegance is at **Neumann** (Seilergasse 3), and the British touch is evident at **Kowalski** (Brandstätte 7–9); rather more 'sophisticated' shops include **Kinki** (Jasomirgottstrasse 5), **Riva** (Kärntnerstrasse 45) and **Firis** (Ruprechtsplatz/Sterngasse). Those who prefer loose, casual clothing shop at **Mac's** (Brandstätte 7–9), **Stefanel** (Haas-Haus on the Stephansplatz), **Fortuna** (Tuchlauben 12), **In Wear** (Rotenturmstrasse 5–9), **Blaumax** (Fleischmarkt 20) or **Benetton** (Kärntnerstrasse 2 and Graben 36). More unusual casual wear, jeans and American jackets can be found in several boutiques along Judengasse.

Department Stores & Shopping Centres

Vienna's most traditional department stores are **Gerngross** (Mariahilferstrasse 38–40) and **Steffl** (Kärntnerstrasse 19). A few metres further on from Gerngross, at the corner of Amerlingstrasse, stands the **Generali-Center**, renovated in 1990. That same year the **Galleria** on the Landstrasser Haupstrasse in district 3 was also opened, along with the exclusive shops of the **Haas-Haus** on the Stephansplatz; and in district 17, close to the Gürtel, an enterprising architect built the **Lugner-City** shopping centre (1150, Gablenzgasse 5). On the other side of the Danube in the north of the city is the **Donauzentrum** (U1), while **Shopping City Süd**, a large shopping complex, is found in the south.

Hairdressers

Everyone from pop stars and journalists to advertising reps and junior bankers go to **Erich** (Griechengasse 7). Also popular are the brothers **Bundy & Bundy** (Habsburgergasse 3), who have been around a long time, and the **Gruppa l'ultima** (Köllnerhofgasse 3), who are known for chic styling. For very elegant styling visit **Ramé** (Walfischgasse 2) and **Grecht** (1030 Spitalgasse 33).

Dry-Cleaning

Stross (Hoher Markt 2) have a 24-hour dry-cleaning service.

Tea

Connoisseur teas and a wide range of useful and beautiful teatime accoutrements can be found at **Schönbichler** (Wollzeile 5), founded in 1870, and at **Jäger** (Operngasse 6); there is also a large selection of teas at **Haas & Haas** (Stephansplatz 4) and at **Demmer's Teehaus** (Mölkerbastei 5).

Wine

Wine lovers will find plenty to tempt them as they wander through the old vault at **Grams & Co** (Singerstrasse 26). Also to be recommended are the **Vinothek St Stephan** (Stephansplatz 6), which also provides a range of select olive oils, **Zum Finsteren Stern** (Sterngasse 6) and the **Vinothek bei der Piaristenkirche** (1080, Piaristengasse 54).

Cakes & Confectionery

The world-famous *Sachertorte* can be obtained at Philharmonikerstrasse 4, at the entrance to Kärntnerstrasse, and its 'competitors', along with very beautifully packaged confectionery, at **Demel** (Kohlmarkt 14). *Imperial-Torte* (Emperor Cake) is on sale at the Bristol and Imperial hotels; Vienna's latest cake creation, the triangular *Domspitz*, can be enjoyed at the **Do & Co** Café on the seventh floor of the Haas-Haus on the Stephansplatz. Cake lovers will find everything they want in the long established Gerstner (Kärntnerstrasse 15) and Heiner (Kärntnerstrasse 21 and Wollzeile 9). The Kurkonditorei Oberlaa (Neuer Markt 16) also has a fine range – from chocolates to Joghurttörtchen (yoghurt-cake).

Fine Belgian chocolates can be bought at **Godiva** (Graben 17) and at **Fabienne** (Wollzeile 5); and **Altmann & Kühne** (Graben 30) sell Viennese chocolate specialities packed in pretty boxes.

Gourmet Fare & Luxury Snacks

Vienna's top address for gourmets is **Meinl am Graben** (Graben 19), and hot and cold snacks are served at the rear of the store in the restaurant (Monday to Saturday 8.30am–11pm and Sunday 11am–3pm. The delicatessens and snack-bars at the **Schwarzes Kameel** (Bognergasse 5), at **Wild** (Neuer Markt 10) and **Böhle** (Wollzeile 30) are all very traditional. Gourmet food and tasty snacks, where the emphasis is on fish and seafood, can be found at **Do & Co** (Akademiestrasse 3), and excellent Italian food is offered by **Da Conte** in Kurrentgasse 12, **Piccini** near the Naschmarkt (1060, Linke Wienzeile 4) and the tiny **Urbanek** restaurant at the Naschmarkt.

Many different and delicious types of bread can be found at the marvellous old **Grimm** bakery (Kurrentgasse 10).

Mall walking

Eating Out

The boom in pub custom in the early 1980s also gave the Viennese gastronomic scene a great deal more variety. The home of 'Viennese Cuisine' – the only cuisine in the world to be named after a city rather than a region or an entire country – is the *Beisl*, a comfortable, usually family-run tavern, where people stand at the *Schank* (bar) with an *Achterl* (an eighth of a litre) of wine or a beer, waiting for a free table. There's usually a *Stammtisch* too (a table reserved for regulars). This particular Viennese institution has been given a new lease of life, and there are several varieties, ranging from the genuine old *Wirtshaus* to the new and stylish *Edelbeisl*.

Just like the Viennese soul, the city's cuisine is a mixture of influences from the original member countries of the Habsburg empire: the famed *Wiener Schnitzel* (traditionally veal, and served with potato salad) is actually of Byzantine descent, and the argument about whether Field Marshal Radetzky took the breadcrumbed speciality with him to Lombardy or returned to Vienna with the recipe for *costoletta milanese* is still a matter of debate. *Gulasch* comes from Hungary (where it is referred to as *pörkölt*), as does *Palatschinken*; the famous desserts *Marillenknödel*, *Apfelstrudel* and *Powidltascherln* are of Bohemian origin. Most dishes containing *Kraut* (cabbage) came from Poland originally, and even the very popular *Schinkenfleckerln* can't conceal the fact that it is descended from Italian pasta.

The Danube's equivalent of nouvelle cuisine is called 'Neue Wiener Küche', a combination of nouvelle cuisine and Viennese specialities robbed of their calories and adapted to contemporary needs.

There are roughly 5,000 places to eat in Vienna, to suit every purse and every taste, ranging from the *Hassn* (a hot sausage eaten while standing up at a sausage stall) to the most sophisticated gourmet restaurant. The following selection reflects this and includes all kinds of eateries, from Viennese institutions to recommended ethnic restaurants, characterful coffee houses and places to go for a late-night snack. Most of the recommendations in the restaurant section are in the moderate price band (500–1,000öS for three courses plus half a litre of wine for two people). Restaurants where prices are noticeably cheaper or more expensive are noted as such.

Restaurants
Viennese Cuisine

ZUR GOLDENEN GLOCKE
1050, Kettenbrückengasse 9
Tel: 587 57 67
Monday to Saturday 11am–2.30pm and 5.30pm–midnight.
Rustic *Beisl* with a beautiful garden, catches the flea-market crowd.

GRÜNAUER
1070, Hermanngasse 32
Tel: 526 40 80
Friday to Tuesday 11.30am–3pm, 6pm–midnight.
Beisl with reasonably priced traditional Viennese specialities. Best to book a table.

ZU DEN DREI HACKEN
1010, Singerstrasse 28
Tel: 512 58 95
Monday to Saturday 10am–midnight.
Rustic Viennese restaurant with traditional Styrian-influenced cuisine.

ZUM HERKNER
1170, Dornbacher Strasse 123
Tel: 485 43 86
Monday to Friday 10.30am–10pm.
Beautiful old Edelbeisl serving good traditional fare, with *Schanigarten* in the summer. It gets very busy, so book a table!

ERDINGER WEISSBIERSTÜBERL
1010, Fleischmarkt 9
Tel: 533 28 73
Monday to Saturday 11am–1am.
Large *Beisl* with generous portions of reasonably priced plain fare.

OFENLOCH
1010, Kurrentgasse 8
Tel: 533 72 68
Daily 10am–midnight,
Traditional Viennese cuisine, located in a medieval vaulted cellar.

PFUDL
1010, Bäckerstrasse 22
Tel: 512 67 05
Monday to Sunday 9am–2am
Venerable old *Edelbeisl* serving enormous portions.

ZUM SCHWARZEN ADLER
1050, Schönbrunner Strasse 40
Tel: 544 11 09, 544 71 74
Tuesday to Saturday 11.30am–2.30pm and 6pm–midnight.
On the expensive side; excellent fish and meat specialities.

SMUTNY
1010, Elisabethstrasse 8
Tel: 587 13 56
Daily
10am–1am
Traditional Viennese cuisine.

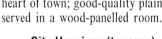

STADTBEISL
1010, Naglergasse 21
Tel: 533 35 07
Daily 10am–midnight.
Old Viennese *Beisl* in the heart of town; good-quality plain fare served in a wood-panelled room.

City Heuriger (taverns)

FIGLMÜLLER
1010, Wollzeile 5 (arcade)
Tel: 512 61 77
Daily 11am–10.30pm
Famous for its gigantic portions of Schnitzel.

AUGUSTINER-KELLER
1010, Augustinerstrasse 1
Tel: 533 10 26
Open daily 11am–midnight
Centuries-old restaurant serving traditional Viennese food.

Fish Restaurants

FISCHRESTAURANT WINTER
1110, Alberne Hafenzufahrtsstrasse 262
Tel: 767 23 17-0
Monday to Saturday noon–10pm.
Near the Danube, with garden and view over the river. First-class food.

KORNAT
1010, Marc-Aurel-Strasse 8
Tel: 535 65 18
Monday to Saturday 11.30am–3pm and 6pm–midnight.
Small, simple and tasteful, on the edge of the Bermuda Triangle.

KERVANSARAY-HUMMER-BAR
1010, Mahlerstrasse 9
Tel: 512 88 43
Monday to Saturday noon–midnight.
Fine restaurant, famous for lobsters and saltwater fish.

Gourmet Restaurants

ALTWIENERHOF
1150, Herklotzgasse 6
Tel: 892 60 00
Monday to Friday 11am–2pm, 6pm–2am, Saturday 6pm–2am.
Top French cuisine; exceptional wine cellar; winter garden. Expensive.

ZU DEN DREI HUSAREN
1010, Weihburggasse 4
Tel: 512 10 92
Daily noon–3pm and 6pm–midnight.
Viennese haute cuisine. Jacket and tie obligatory. Expensive.

For fast food

KORSO IM HOTEL BRISTOL
1010, Mahlerstrasse 2
Tel: 515 16 546
Monday to Sunday noon–3pm, 6–1am, Saturday 6pm–1am.
Reinhard Gerer creates the finest cuisine in town. Elegant and expensive.

SCHWARZENBERG
1030, Schwarzenbergplatz 9
Tel: 798 45 15-620
Daily noon–2.30pm and 6–11pm.
Elegant restaurant in the Palais Schwarzenberg. Great views from the Winter Gardens into the private sections of the palace. Very high prices.

STEIRERECK
1030, Rasumofskygasse 2
Tel: 713 31 68
Monday to Friday noon–3pm, 7–11.30pm.
New Viennese cuisine from one of the best cooks in the city. High class and therefore expensive.

Fashionable Restaurants

APROPOS
1010, Rudolfsplatz 12
Tel: 533 41 89
Monday to Wednesday 8pm–4am, Thursday to Saturday 6pm–4am, Sunday 6pm–2am.
Favoured by the young and hip.

CREPERIE AM SPITTELBERG
1070, Spittelbergggasse 12
Tel: 526 15 70
Open daily 6pm–midnight (*Schanigarten* until 10pm).
Cosy pub at the Spittelberg; French crêpes, health food. Outdoor seating in summer.

DO & CO IM HAAS-HAUS
1010, Stephansplatz 12
Tel: 535 39 69
Open daily noon–3pm and 6pm–midnight.

Viennese cuisine, lobster and oysters, plus Vienna's most beautiful view.

PRINZ FERDINAND
1080, Bennoplatz 2
Tel: 402 94 17
Open daily 11.30am–3pm, 5.30pm–midnight.
Light Viennese cuisine and excellent wine list; delightful *Schanigarten*.

LUSTHAUS
1020, Prater, Freudenau 254
Tel: 728 95 65
Saturday, Sunday noon–6pm, Tuesday, Thursday, Friday noon–11pm. In winter only open at weekends. Romantic pavilion in the middle of Prater's woods; best in summer on the open terrace. Excellent food.

MA PITOM
1010, Seitenstettengasse 5
Tel: 535 43 13
Sunday to Thursday 5pm–1am, Friday and Saturday 5pm–2am.
Restaurant with *Schanigarten*.

OSWALD & KALB
1010, Bäckerstrasse 14
Tel: 512 13 71
Daily 6pm–12.30am.
Excellent Viennese-Styrian cuisine. Popular meeting place for artists, media people and politicians.

ENRICO PANIGL
1080, Josefstädter Strasse 91
Tel: 406 52 18
Open daily 6pm–2am.
Old restaurant; large choice of pasta dishes; good wine list.

SALZAMT
1010, Ruprechtsplatz 1
Tel: 533 53 32
Daily noon–2am.
The best restaurant in the Bermuda Triangle. For all

cool people as well as those who like to think they are. Postmodernist styling.

SANTO SPIRITO
1010, Kumpfgasse 7
Tel: 512 99 98
Monday to Thursday 11am–2am; Friday and Saturday 11am–1am; Sunday 10am–2am.
Convivial restaurant where classical musicians stroll among the tables. Classical and baroque music.

SCHNATTL
1080, Langegasse 40
Tel: 405 34 00
Monday to Friday 11.30am–2.30pm, 6pm–midnight, Saturday 6pm–midnight.
Elegant and cosy atmosphere, very good Styrian cuisine; quite expensive.

African

SAGYA
1090, Liechtensteinstrasse 130a
Tel: 310 90 99
Monday to Friday 9am–midnight, Saturday 5pm–2am.
Recommended for its exotic food. Moderate prices.

Arabian

AL BADAUI
1010 Habsburgergasse 12a
Tel: 533 79 25
Open daily 6pm–midnight, in the summer also at midday.
Arabian Nights atmosphere. Classical Styrian-Palestinian cuisine.

Bar flies

Brazilian

MICHL'S CHURRASCARIA
1150, Sechshauserstrasse 76
Tel: 893 61 07
Daily 6pm–midnight.
A large choice of meat dishes.

Chinese

KIANG
1010, Rotgasse 8
Tel: 533 08 56
Monday to Saturday 11.30am–11.30pm, Sunday 6pm–1am.
Tasty dishes. Extremely stylish and highly praised decor.

PANDA
1070 Westbahnstrasse 35
Tel: 526 94 88
Daily 11.30am–11pm.
Tiny family-run restaurant offering very good food; no fake Chinese decor. Inexpensive.

French

SALUT
1010 Wildpretmarkt 3
Tel: 533 35 81
Tuesday to Saturday 11.30am–2pm, 6–11pm.
Elegant ambience, innovative French cuisine. Try the bouillabaisse, snails, fois gras and crêpes.

Greek

DER GRIECHE PANOS TSATSARIS
1060, Barnabitengasse 5
Tel: 587 74 66, 587 01 80
Daily 11.30am–3pm, 6pm–midnight.
Regarded by Vienna's Greek community as the best in town.

SCHWARZE KATZE
1060, Girardigasse 6
Tel: 587 06 25
Tuesday to Sunday 6.30pm–1am.
Moussaka, tsatziki etc. Inexpensive, but delicious.

Hungarian

ILONA-STÜBERL
1010, Bräunerstrasse 2
Tel: 533 90 29
Monday to Saturday noon–3pm and 6–11pm.
Small restaurant with Hungarian specialities. Reasonable prices.

Indian

MAHARADSCHA
1010, Gölsdorfgasse 1
Tel: 533 74 43
Daily 11.30am–2.30pm and 6–11pm.
The best Indian restaurant in town.

Italian

AL CAVALLINO
1010, Dorotheergasse 19
Tel: 512 39 36
Monday to Saturday 11.30am–2.30pm and 6–11pm.
Popular pizzeria with rustic atmosphere.

GROTTA AZZURRA
1010, Babenbergerstrasse 5
Tel: 586 10 44
Open daily noon–3pm, 6.30pm–11pm.
Famous Italian restaurant with classical furniture and Venetian paintings. Live Italian music on Sundays.

DA LUCIANO
1070, Sigmundsgasse 14
Tel: 523 77 78
Wednesday to Sunday noon–3pm, 6.30pm–11.30pm.
High-class establishment popular with the glitterati.

LA TAVERNETTA
1070, Burggasse 44
Tel: 523 47 47
Tuesday to Saturday noon–2.30pm, 6.30–11pm. Sunday noon–2.30pm.
Fine Italian food, especially fresh fish. Expensive.

OLIVA VERDE
1080, Florianigasse 15
Tel: 405 41 06
Monday to Friday noon–3pm, 6pm–midnight.
Health food bias, decently furnished and with an ambitious cook.

Japanese

K2
1010, Fleischmarkt 6
Tel: 535 68 28
Open daily noon–2.30pm, 6–11pm.
Vienna's best sushi bar.

TENMAYA
1010, Krugerstrasse 3
Tel: 512 73 97
Daily 11.30am–3pm, 5pm–midnight.
High-class Japanese restaurant with excellent cuisine, Sushi bar and Tatami rooms. Expensive.

Jewish

ARCHE NOAH
1010, Seitenstettengasse 2
Tel: 533 13 74
Monday to Friday 11.30am–3.30pm, 6.30–11pm, Saturday 11.30am–2.30pm (November to April also 6.30–11pm on Saturday).
Best kosher restaurant in town, located located in the Bermuda Triangle.

Korean

OSTWIND
1070, Lindengasse 24
Tel: 523 41 82
Daily 11.30am–2.30pm and 5.30pm–midnight.
Korean, Chinese and Japanese specialities. Reasonable prices.

Russian

FEUERVOGEL
1090, Alserbachstrasse 21
Tel: 317 53 91–01

Monday to Saturday 6pm–noon.
This elegant restaurant has been Vienna's top Russian establishment for over 70 years. Come here for all the favourite staples of the Russian menu: *borscht*, caviar, *blini*, as well as more substantial fare.

Serbian

BEOGRAD
1040, Schikanedergasse 5
Tel: 587 74 44
Thursday to Tuesday 11.30am–1.30am
Balkan specialities; garden open until 10pm.

Spanish

PEDRO'S MESON
1070, Siebensterngasse 5
Tel: 523 99 85

Monday to Saturday 6pm–1am.
Small and cosy.

Turkish

LEVANTE
1080, Josefstädterstrasse 14
Tel: 408 53 06, 409 82 36
1010, Wallnerstrasse 2
Tel: 533 23 26
Daily 11.30am–11.30pm.
Great kebab and vegetable specialities. Inexpensive.

SARIKOC
1090 Währingerstrasse 18
Tel: 319 99 87
Daily 11am–midnight.
Fine Turkish food, accompanied by belly dancing.

Vegetarian

WRENKH
1010, Bauernmarkt 10
Tel: 533 15 26, 535 33 62 (Bar)
Restaurant: Open daily 11am–11pm.
Bar: 11am–1am.
Vienna's best vegetarian restaurant; a welcome escape from pork and potatoes.

Coffee Houses

ALT WIEN
1010, Bäckerstrasse 9
Tel: 512 52 22
Daily 10am–2am, Friday and Saturday until 4am.

BRÄUNERHOF
1010, Stallburggasse 2
Tel: 512 38 93
Monday to Friday 7.30am–8.30pm, Saturday 7.30am–7pm and Sunday 10am–7pm.

CENTRAL
1010, Herrengasse 14
(Palais Ferstel).
Tel: 533 37 63–26
Monday to Saturday 8am–10pm.

Fresh ingredients

DIGLAS
1010, Wollzeile 10
Tel: 512 84 01
Daily 7am–midnight.

FRAUENHUBER
1010, Himmelpfortgasse 6
Tel: 512 43 23
Monday to Saturday 8am–midnight, Sunday 10am–10pm.

GRIENSTEIDL
1010 Michaelerplatz 2
Tel: 535 26 92
Daily 8am–midnight.

HAWELKA
1010, Dorotheergasse 12
Tel: 512 82 30
Monday and Wednesday to Saturday 8am–2am, Sunday and holidays 4pm–2am. Closed Tuesday.

KLEINES CAFÉ
1010, Franziskanerplatz 3
Monday to Saturday 10am–2am
Sunday 1pm–2am.

LANDTMANN
1010, Dr Karl-Lueger-Ring 4
Tel: 532 06 21
Daily 8am–midnight.

MUSEUM
1010, Friedrichstrasse 6
Tel: 586 52 02
Daily 8am–midnight.

SALZGRIES
1010, Marc-Aurel-Strasse 6
Tel: 533 54 26
Monday to Friday 8am–1am, Saturday, Sunday and holidays noon–1am.

SPERL
1060, Gumpendorfer Strasse 11
Tel: 586 41 58
Monday to Saturday 7am–11pm, Sunday 3–11pm.

STEIN
1090 Währingerstrasse 6–8
Tel: 319 72 41
Monday to Saturday 7am–1am, Sunday 9am–1am.
Chic student/literary and in-crowd café with mix of new cuisine and favourite standbys.

Snacks

LUSTIG ESSEN
1010, Salvatorgasse 6
Tel: 533 30 37
Daily 11.30am–11pm.
Mini portions of Viennese and international specialities – eat your way through the menu.

KOLAR
1010, Kleeblattgasse 5
Tel: 533 52 25
Open daily 5pm–2am.
The house speciality is a pitta sandwich cooked in a wood-fired oven. Smoky and lively.

TRZESNIEWSKI
1010, Dorotheergasse 1
Tel: 512 32 91
Monday to Friday 9am–7.30pm, Saturday 8.30am–5pm (every first Saturday in the month until 6pm.)
Sandwiches and rolls with spicy fillings.

Fashionable Bars

Vienna's nightlife begins late, but that makes it all the more intensive.

REISS CHAMPAGNERTREFF
1010, Marco d'Aviano-Gasse 1
Tel: 512 71 98
Monday to Friday 11am–3am, Saturday 10am–3am, Sunday 11am–2am.
Very stylish and rather posh.

CAFÉ-BAR IN DER SEZESSION
1010, Friedrichstrasse 12

Tel: 586 93 86
Tuesday to Sunday 6pm–2am.
Colourful downstairs pub.

EDEN
1010, Liliengasse 2
Tel: 512 74 50
Open daily 10pm–4am.
Vienna's nicest Plüschbar, with an elderly clientele. Jacket and tie obligatory.

ONYX BAR
1010, Stephensplatz (Haas and Haus)
Tel: 535 39 69–429
Monday to Saturday 9am–2am, Sunday 9am–6pm.
On the 6th floor, opposite St Stephen's cathedral; great view.

CASTILLO
1010, Biberstrasse 8
Tel: 512 71 23
Monday to Saturday 8pm–3am, Sunday 8pm–2am.

PLANTER'S CLUB
1010, Zelinkagasse 4
Tel: 533 33 93–15
Open daily 5pm–4am.
Fantastic, 'tropical' ambience.

OSWALD & KALB
1010, Bäckerstrasse 14
Tel: 512 13 71
Open daily 6pm–2am.
Despite the competition, Oswald & Kalb remains one of Vienna's most popular bars.

The place for a night-cap

SALZAMT

1010, Ruprechtsplatz 1
Tel: 533 53 32
Open daily noon–2am.
Superbly designed pub and bar in the Bermuda Triangle.

Internet-cafés

G-ZONE

1010, Universitätsstrasse 11/3
Tel: 407 81 66
www.g-zone.at
Monday to Friday 10am–11pm, Saturday, Sunday and holidays 2–11pm.
28 computers in total, ATS 1.-/min.

Einstein

1010, Rathausplatz 4
Tel: 405 26 26
www.einstein.at
Monday to Friday 7–2am, Saturday 9–2am, Sunday and holidays 9am–midnight.
4 computers, ATS 1.90/min.

A lively bar scene

Bignet

1010, Hoher Markt 8–9
Tel: 533 29 39
www.bignet.at
Open daily 10am–midnight
18 computers, ATS 2.-/min.

Live Music

NEUER ENGEL

1010, Rabensteig 5
Tel: 535 41 05
Monday to Thursday 5pm–2am, Friday, Saturday 5pm–4am, Sunday 6pm–2am.
Design by Coop Himmelblau; live music every night; billiards.

JAZZLAND

1010, Franz Josephs-Kai 29
Tel: 533 25 75
Monday to Saturday 7pm–2am.
Daily live jazz from 9pm; hot dishes and snacks.

HAVANNA CLUB

1010, Mahlerstrasse 11
Tel: 513 20 75
Latino and Caribbean Jazz.

PAPAS TAPAS

1040, Schwarzenbergplatz 10
Tel: 505 03 11
Monday to Saturday 8pm–1.30am.
Large pub offering good *tapas* and live music.

Nightclubs

OLYMPIA STUDIOS

1010, Rotgasse 9
Tel: 535 99 95
Open daily 10pm–4am.
This is the largest disco in the central area. Very young crowd.

U4

1120, Schönbrunnerstrasse 222
(U4 Parkshop Meidling)
Tel: 815 83 07
Open daily 10pm–4am.
Disco with hip appeal, gloomy, but a hot spot.

NACHTWERK

1230, Dr Gonda-Gasse 9

Laxenburgerstrasse
Tel: 616 88 80
Friday and Saturday 9pm–5am.
Large disco on the edge of town;
lasers, mega sound system and giant
video screen.

VOLKSGARTEN
1010, Volksgarten (U3)
Tel: 533 05 18
Mon 10pm–5am, Tue, Wed
10pm–4am, Thu 8pm–2am, Fri, Sat
8pm–5am, Sun 5pm–4am.
1950s atmosphere; dancing outside
in the summer; Monday night special: 'Soul Seduction'.

QUEEN ANNE
1010, Johannesgasse 12
Tel: 513 95 03
Sunday to Thursday 10pm–4am, Friday and Saturday until 6am.
Cocktail bar frequented by the beautiful people.

Cabaret

METROPOL
1170, Hernalser Hauptstrasse 55
Tel: 407 77 40–7
Cabaret and music programmes; open-
air theatre in the summer.

SPEKTAKEL
1050, Hamburgerstrasse 14
Tel: 587 06 23
Cabaret and *Beisl.*

KULISSE
1170, Rosensteingasse 39
Tel: 485 38 70
Cabaret and music; cosy *Beisl.*

NIEDERMAIR
1080, Lenaugasse 1a
Tel: 408 44 92
Young cabaret and satire; 'Kabarett-
Beisl Niedermeierei' is located just next
door.

Eating for Night Owls

SALZ & PFEFFER
1060, Joanelligasse 8
Tel: 586 66 60

Music man

Sunday to Thursday 6pm–8am,
Saturday 6pm–9am.
Serves plain fare and international
cuisine.

CAFÉ DRECHSLER
1060, Link Wienzeile 22
Tel: 587 85 80
Monday to Friday 3am–8pm, Satur-
day 3am–6pm.
Popular meeting place for early birds.
Very Viennese, but not for the health-
conscious: it's thick with smoke.

NOODLES & CO
1010 Karlsplatz 5
(in the basement of the Künstlerhaus)
Tel: 505 38 39
Sunday to Friday 11am–3pm,
6pm–2am, Saturday 6pm–2am.
Convivial restaurant serving mainly
Italian food. Offers live piano music
from 9pm.

EUROPA
1070 Zollergasse 8
Tel: 526 3383
Daily 9am–5am.
Attracts a cool, trendy clientele, and
the food is satisfying.

TRAVEL ESSENTIALS

When to Visit

The temperature can fluctuate between 15 and 35°C in August, and between 5 and -22C in January. The one thing you can rely on unfailingly is the wind: it blows at least 200 days a year. Normally, spring and autumn are the best times to visit Vienna. The clear light in autumn, after the summer haze, is particularly beautiful. Rain protection and a warmish jacket are always a good idea.

Driving in the City

In Vienna, the same applies as for other large cities: leave your car in the hotel garage. Above all, make sure you avoid the city centre within the Ringstrasse; even taxi drivers have trouble coping with the continually changing system of one-way streets.

See *Orientation* (page 22) for information on how to reach the city centre from the various motorways.

By Train

Vienna has two main railway stations: the Westbahnhof and the Südbahnhof.
Westbahnhof
1150, Mariahilfergürtel/Mariahilfer- strasse (U6, Tram Nos 5,6,9,18) fo all destinations in Western Austria Germany, France, Switzerland, etc.
Südbahnhof
1040, Wiener Gürtel 1 (Bus 13A, U1 S-Bahn, Tram Nos O, D, 18) for des tinations in Southern Austria, Italy the former Yugoslavia, etc.
Bahnhof Wien-Mitte
1030, Landstrasser Hauptstrasse (S Bahn, U4, U3, Tram O, Bus 74A) fo destinations to the north and north east of Vienna.
Wien-Nord/Praterstern
1020, Praterstern (U1, S-Bahn, Tram Nos 1, 5, O, Bus 80A) for connec tions to Northern Austria.
Franz-Josephs-Bahnhof
1090, Julius-Tandler-Platz 9 (Tram D, 5, near the U4). This station ha lost a lot of its former importance most departures from here are to East ern Austria and the Czech and Slo vak republics.

As well as in the stations themselves seats can be reserved in the city cen tre at the Österreichische Verkehrs büro, or Austrian Tourist Office (1010 Friedrichstrasse 7, Monday to Friday 8.30am–5.30pm); the Südbahnhof an the Westbahnhof also have a Bahn hofsreisebüro, or station travel office

which looks after things like bookings, tickets, timetables, etc.
'Bahntotalservice'
Tel: 05 17 17 (daily 4am–10pm)
Central Train Information
Tel: 05 17 17

If you are planning to travel a lot in Austria or to destinations in neighbouring countries (Munich, Prague, etc), consider buying a Vorteilskarte for 1,290öS (passport photo required), which allows 50 percent discount on all trips in Austria for a year (two round trips to Innsbruck, for instance, will pay for it).

By Air

Wien-Schwechat airport lies roughly 19km (12 miles) southeast of Vienna. It was built in 1960 and has been undergoing extension work since the end of the 1980s.

By car it takes around 30 minutes to get from the city centre to the airport, via Franz-Josephs-Kai and the airport *Autobahn*, but the early morning and evening traffic jams before joining the *Autobahn* can increase the time considerably.

Express buses run from the City Air Terminal, Hilton-Stadtpark (near the U3, U4) to the airport daily 5am–midnight (round the clock between April and October) every 30 minutes. Journey time 30–50 minutes. There are also airport buses from the Westbahnhof and the Südbahnhof (departures hourly; journey time 50 minutes; price for both services is 70öS).

A few radio taxis (eg, tel: 31 300) offer discounts if taxis are ordered in advance.

In general the banks are open Monday to Friday 8am–12.30pm and 1.30–3pm (Thursday until 5.30pm). The head offices of several financial institutions stay open at lunchtime, too (eg Creditanstalt, 1010, Schottengasse 1; Erste Österreichische, 1010, Graben 21; Zentralsparkasse, 1030, Vordere Zollamtsstrasse 13).

There is also a comprehensive network of automatic teller machines, many of which are connected to the international banking system.
Südbahnhof: Daily 6.30am–10pm
Westbahnhof: Daily 7am–10pm
Airport (exchange office): departure hall daily 6am–8.30pm; arrival hall daily 8am–11pm
Air Terminal/Hilton Hotel: Daily 8am–12.30pm and 2–6pm
öAMTC **Touring Centre West:** Currency exchange daily 7am–6pm (1140, Hadikgasse 128, in the direction of the Westautobahn)
Currency Exchange: Stephansplatz (daily 9am–5.30pm), Opernpassage (daily 8am–7pm)
City centre automatic tellers include:
Stephansplatz 2
Kärntner Strasse 51 (opposite the Staatsoper)
Franz-Josephs-Kai 21/Schwedenplatz
Schottengasse 10

Geography and Topography

Austria's federal capital of Vienna is also the smallest of the country's nine federal states and has 1.6 million inhabitants.

As far as its landscape is concerned, the west of Vienna belongs to the Northern Vienna Woods, then come the mountainous Alpine foothills, the Viennese tableland, the Danube meadows and the flat alluvial plain of the

Marchfeld. The north, including the Bisamberg, is already part of Weinviertler Hügelland. Vienna lies at an average of 172 metres (564ft) above sea-level; the highest point is the Hermannskogel (542 metres/1,778ft) in the northwest, and the lowest point is in the Lobau by the Danube (150 metres/490ft).

The surface area of the city is approximately 414.5 sq km (160 sq miles). A walk round the city's borders would be roughly 130km (80 miles) long.

Districts

1. Innere Stadt **2.** Leopoldstadt **3.** Landstrasse **4.** Wieden **5.** Margareten **6.** Mariahilf **7.** Neubau **8.** Josefstadt **9.** Alsergrund **10.** Favoriten **11.** Simmering **12.** Meidling **13.** Hietzing **14.** Penzing **15.** Rudolfsheim-Fünfhaus **16.** Ottkaring **17.** Hernals **18.** Währing **19.** Döbling **20.** Brigittenau **21.** Floridsdorf **22.** Donaustadt **23.** Liesing

Climate and Viewing Points

Vienna lies on the border between the continental temperate climate and the oceanic climate. The average temperature is minus 1.4°C in January (when temperatures can vary between -22 and 5°C), and 19 °C at the height of summer (variations from 15–35°C). Approximately 600mm (23½ inches) of rain falls annually, spread throughout the seasons relatively uniformly. On clear days, especially in spring and late autumn, the following places offer the best views:

Leopoldsberg: 425m (1,400ft), the northernmost part of the Kahlenberg range; the medieval fortress tower on the summit, restored after 1945, provides a wonderful view of Vienna and the Danube.

Kahlenberg: The 484-m (1,587-ft) high neighbouring mountain of the

Leopoldsberg affords a magnificent view of the city (observation terrace).

Hermannskogel: This mountain, the highest point in Vienna (542m/1,778ft), lies to the northwest of the city; there's a great view of the city to be had from here.

Donauturm: To the north of the Danube, the Donaupark and the 252-metre (826-ft) high Donauturm (Danube Tower) were constructed as part of the International Garden Exhibition in 1964; the revolving top floor has a café and a restaurant with magnificent views, if only average food.

St Stephen's Cathedral/Stephansplatz: Access to the express lift up to the Nordturm (North Tower) is on the left side-aisle of the cathedral; open daily from 9am–6pm. Access to the Südturm (South Tower) which is 137m (450ft) high is on the outside of the Cathedral; open daily 9am–5.30pm.

Haas-Haus/Stephansplatz: The café on the seventh floor provides the finest

view of the colourful roof-tiles of the cathedral. There is also a particularly fine view to be had from the terrace of the restaurant next door, Do & Co, only accessible to restaurant guests).

Vienna and Foreigners

The Viennese attitude to foreigners is double-edged. They like them in small doses and are happy to provide them with information. Large concentrations of tourists make them nervous, especially if they happen to be carousing loudly. In the first district, the Viennese take foreigners in their stride.

GETTING AROUND

Maps

Most bookstores and kiosks in the city centre sell small plans of the city and guides to Vienna. There's a particularly comprehensive selection of maps and city guides at **Freytag & Berndt**, 1010, Kohlmarkt 9.

Round Trips

CITYRAMA SIGHTSEEING REISEBÜRO
1010, Börsegasse 1, tel: 534 13-0
HOP ON HOP OFF
Tel: 712 46 83–0
Regular bus service with 13 stops, daily every hour 9am–7.30pm.

Round Trips by Boat

Between the end of March and the end of October the DDSG (Donaudampfschiffahrtsgesellschaft) offers a variety of round trips and outings by boat.

For information, contact DDSG, 1010, Friedrichsstrasse 7, tel: 588 80 –440.

Fiaker *(Horse-Drawn Cabs)*

The Viennese *fiaker* were at their most popular in the 18th and 19th centuries: at that time there were more than 1,000 of these picturesque horse-drawn cabs in the city. Around three dozen of them remain today, and they are mainly used to take tourists around the city centre. As with the gondoliers in Venice, it is recommended that you agree on a fixed price before starting your journey; the main 'cab ranks' can be found on the Heldenplatz and on Stephansplatz.

Guided Tours

For those interested in the less well-known aspects of Vienna, the *Wiener Stadtspaziergänge*, or 'Walks through Vienna', offers over three dozen different routes on various themes, such as 'Crime Legends of Old Vienna', 'The Vienna of *The Third Man*', 'Jugendstil', or 'On the Trail of Mozart'. Each tour is accompanied by a trained guide, costs around 140öS and takes about 90 minutes to complete. A free brochure on these tours can be found at Tourist Information (1010, Albertinaplatz, www.wienguide.at).

In the summer months the *Reisebuchladen* (Travel Book Shop) organises alternative guided tours of Vienna with a critical edge (information: 1090 Kolingasse 6, tel: 317 33 84).

Public Transport

The quickest way to get around Vienna is to take one of the five U-Bahn lines. Taking trams and buses can result in long waits in the early morning and evening, and after 8pm. The trams and the U-Bahn generally start at 5am and go on until midnight, while the buses (apart from the City-Buses) start at 6.30am and go on until midnight .For information, call 790 91 05.

The so-called City-Buses in District 1 are a very comfortable way to travel. A disadvantage, though, is that they only run until 8pm on weekdays, and until 2pm on Saturdays (although on the first Saturday of every month and on the four Saturdays before Christmas they run until 5pm).

Night Buses

On the nights preceding national holidays and Sundays, eight night bus routes run between 12.30am and 4am

from Schwedenplatz. The good news: it's a great way of getting home cheaply in the middle of the night. The bad news: the journey time is relatively long, because the buses have to go right round all the most important districts.

A one-way-trip costs 15öS; tickets are obtained from automatic machines inside the bus. The precise times of departure and routing are available in a free brochure available at information centres of the Wiener Verkehrsbetrieb (eg U-Bahn station Karlsplatz, Monday to Friday 6.30am–6.30pm, Saturday, Sunday, public holidays 8.30am–4pm).

Tickets & Travel Regulations

The different forms of public transport are all part of the VOR (Verkehrsverbund Ostregion). This means you are entitled to use just one ticket to travel by bus, U-Bahn, tram and S-Bahn, the only condition being that you must not break your journey for any length of time, and must travel in one logical direction.

Single tickets are sold on buses and trams as well as from automatic machines in U-Bahn and S-Bahn stations.

A cheaper way of doing things is to buy one of the 24-hour, 72-hour or weekly network tickets, sold in most tobacconist shops (Tabak Trafik) and Vienna Transport ticket offices.

Advance sales outlets:
1010, U-Bahn station Stephansplatz
1010, U-Bahn station Karlsplatz
1010, U-Bahn station Schwedenplatz
(Opening times: Monday to Friday 6.30am–6.30pm)

Tickets:
Vorverkaufsfahrschein: Can only be bought in blocks of five at a time.
8-Tage-Umwelt-Streifennetzkarte: These are valid for eight days of your choice; can also be used by more than one person.

7-Tage Netzkarte: Valid for seven days.
Netzkarte 72 Stunden Wien: Valid for as many trips as you like within 72 hours.
Netzkarte 24 Stunden Wien: Valid for as many trips as you like within 24 hours.
Schnupperkarte: Valid for as many trips as you like during the same day, provided they are between 8am and 8pm.

Taxis

It's very easy to get hold of a taxi in Vienna – either wave one down or go to one of the taxi-ranks. Delays are only likely to occur in the morning and evening rush hour, in bad weather and also during the Ball Season (January to February) between midnight and 2am.

A list of all the city's taxi-rank locations can be found on page three of the Vienna phone book.

Prices: Within the Gürtel trips cost between 60 and 100 *schillings*; and there's an extra charge for luggage as well as for evening and weekend journeys. The fixed basic charge is: 26öS

Radio-Taxis:
Tel: 60 160/31 300/81 400/40 106

An extra charge of 26öS is made if you order a cab by telephone though the distance it travels to reach you (minus waiting time) is free of charge.

For taxi rides to the **airport** it's a good idea to state that the radio-taxi has to go 'zum Flughafen' because several of the city's radio cab companies offer a special discount rate on this particular route.

Courier Services:
Blitzkurier: 409 49 49–0
Fahrradbotendienst Veloce (bicycle couriers): 521 17–0

Most taxis will also accept express packages.

Cycling

Vienna has over 300km (180 miles) of cycle paths, though the cycle lanes and part of the pavement reserved for pedestrians are not always very clearly marked, especially in the area around the Ringstrasse and along the Donaukanal. Cyclists and pedestrians should keep a sharp eye out for one another. The cycle paths in the Lobau and through the Prater are particularly attractive thoroughfares, as are the ones along the Donaukanal and the Danube.

You can get a brochure detailing the city's cycle paths from **Stadtinformation** (1080, Town Hall, entrance on Friedrich-Schmidt-Platz, Monday to Friday 6am–6pm; tel: 525 50).

On the U-Bahn system it's possible to travel with a bicycle on Saturdays from 4pm onwards and all day long on Sundays and public holidays; also from May to September, Monday to Friday 9am–3pm and from 6.30pm onwards, and also from 9am onwards on Saturdays.

You can hire a cycle from **Pedal Power**, 1020, Ausstellungsstrasse 3, tel: 729 72 34; 1020, Prater (near the Hochschaubahn), tel: 729 58 88; 1220, Reichsbrücke/neue Donau, tel: 263 52 42.

On Foot

All major sights within the Ringstrasse can easily be visited on foot. The Kärntnerstrasse, the Graben, the Kohlmarkt, the Naglergasse and the Blutgasse are all pedestrian precincts, as is the Spittelberg. But beware: delivery lorries are allowed to drive along these streets until 11am daily.

ACCOMMODATION

Hotels

Whether you choose to stay in Vienna's top luxury hotel, the Palais Schwarzenberg, or opt for a little *Pension*, there will be something in Vienna to suit your taste. The following is a brief selection.

For on-the-spot advice see the list of tourist information offices under

Useful Information, on page 92.

5-Star Luxury Hotels

All Vienna's traditional luxury hotels are situated either on or very near the Ringstrasse:

HOTEL IM PALAIS SCHWARZENBERG
1030, Schwarzenbergplatz 9.
Tel: 798 45 15
44 rooms; doubles from 3,400öS
Palais Schwarzenberg offers truly regal accommodation, in a wing of a baroque palace; some of the rooms enjoy views of the magnificent private park.

HOTEL IMPERIAL
1015 Kärntner Ring 16
Tel: 50 11 00
128 rooms; doubles from 5,500öS.
Voted one of the world's best hotels. Very luxurious.

HOTEL BRISTOL
1015 Kärntner Ring 1,
Tel: 515 160
140 rooms; doubles from 3,950öS.
Hotel Bristol is one of the most famous landmarks on the Ringstrasse, located next to the Opera House. Its

numerous amenities are truly first-class and include the best hotel-restaurant in Vienna.

International Hotel Chains

VIENNA INTER-CONTINENTAL
1030, Johannesgasse 28
Tel: 711 22–0
453 rooms; doubles from 2,100öS. International standard, excellent location next to city parks.

HILTON
1030, Am Stadtpark.
Tel: 717 00–0
600 rooms; doubles from 2,000öS. Usual high standards.

VIENNA MARRIOTT
1010, Parkring 12a
Tel: 515 18–0
313 rooms; doubles from 2,400öS. Postmodern architecture, opposite the Stadtpark.

4-Star Hotels

HOLIDAY INN CROWNE PLAZA
1020, Handelskai 269
Tel: 727 77.
367 rooms; doubles from 1,970öS. A former grain silo on the Danube, converted into a hotel (terrace with view of river).

BIEDERMEIER HOTEL IM SÜNNHOF
1030, Landstrasser Haupstrasse 28
Tel: 716 71–0
203 rooms; doubles from 2,650öS. This peacefully situated hotel occupies a restored Biedermeier building.

CORDIAL THEATERHOTEL
1080, Josefstädterstrasse 22
Tel: 405 36 48
54 rooms; doubles from 2,070öS. Attractive hotel, next to theatre of the same name, only a few minutes away from the Ring.

KÖNIG VON UNGARN
1010, Schulerstrasse 10
Tel: 515 84–0
33 rooms; doubles from 2,000öS. Small traditional hotel in an originally medieval building near the Stephansplatz. Breakfast included.

3-Star Hotels and below

HOTEL WANDL
1010, Petersplatz 9
Tel: 534 55-0
138 rooms; doubles from 1,200öS. Small and comfortable hotel behind the Peterskirche, near the Graben pedestrian precinct.

HOTELPENSION ZIPSER
1080 Lange Gasse 49
Tel: 404 540
50 rooms; doubles from 980öS. Pleasant family hotel situated only a few minutes' walk from the *Rathaus* (Town Hall).

Pensions

ARENBERG
1010, Stubenring 2
Tel: 512 52 91.
22 rooms; doubles from 1480öS. Comfortable 4-star *pension* near the Urania.

NOSSEK
1010, Graben 17
Tel: 533 70 41-0
26 rooms; doubles from 1250öS. There are probably nicer *pensionen* in the city, but none so beautifully located at this price (3-star pension).

Campsites

WIEN-WEST II
1140, Hüttelbergstrasse 80
Tel: 914 23 14
Open from March–January

CAMPING RODAUN
1236, Wien-Rodaun, An der Auz

Tel: 888 41 54
Open from March–November

Camping Information

Camping und Caravaning Club Austria (cca)
1150, Mariahilferstrasse 180.
Tel: 891 21–0

Youth Hostels

Turmherberge Don Bosco
1030, Lechnerstrasse 12
Tel: 713 14 94
50 beds (rooms have more than one bed). One night without breakfast from 80öS. Near the Prater and the Donaukanal, not central, but extremely cheap.

Jugendherberge Myrthengasse
1070, Myrthengasse 7
Tel: 523 03 16
242 beds; bed & breakfast from 170öS. A comfortable youth hostel, near the Spittelberg.

Schlossherberge am Wilhelminenberg
1160, Savoyenstrasse 2
Tel: 485 85 03–700
164 beds (4-bed rooms), bed & breakfast from 220öS. An excellent youth hostel on the edge of the city, in a castle park located close to the Vienna Woods.

BUSINESS HOURS & HOLIDAYS

Shop opening times in Vienna are a recurring bone of contention. Since 1991 shops have been allowed to remain open Monday to Friday until 7.30pm and once a week until 9pm, and until 5pm one Saturday each month. In spite of these new laws, a large number of shops continue to close at 6pm or 6.30pm on weekdays, and at 12 noon or 5pm on Saturday.

Most supermarkets and grocery stores stick to these times too. Exceptions are the Meinl-Gourmet chain on the Opernring which stays open daily until 8pm, and the Billa supermarket chain which stays open until 8pm every Friday and until 5pm every Saturday. Most shops stay open over lunchtime, and many of them remain open until 8pm on Thursdays.

On the last four Saturdays before Christmas, almost every shop is open until 5pm.

Public Holidays

The only public holidays listed here are the ones that can fall on weekdays:
New Year's Day: 1 January

Epiphany: 6 January
Easter Monday
Labour Day *(Staatsfeiertag)*: 1 May
Ascension Day *(Christi Himmelfahrt)*
Whit Monday *(Pfingstmontag)*
Corpus Christi *(Fronleichnam)*
Assumption *(Mariä Himmelfahrt)*
National Holiday *(Nationalfeiertag)*
  26 October
All Saints' Day *(Allerheiligen)*: 1 November
Immaculate Conception *(Mariä*

Empfängnis): 8 December
Christmas Day *(1. Weihnachtstag)*:
25 December
St Stephen's Day *(2. Weihnachtstag)*:
26 December

CRIME

Like any large city, Vienna has its fair share of crime. Take the usual precautions: lock your car, don't leave wallets and other things of value lying around. Prostitution is concentrated along the Gürtel and with it comes the usual twilight world activities. Avoid this area at night on foot. Also to be avoided at night are the 10th and 3rd districts, where bars are often violent

MEDIA

Newspapers & Magazines

The Austrian newspaper market is one of the most comprehensive in the world. The biggest-selling daily paper in the country is the tabloid *Kronen-Zeitung*. The 'Krone', as it is familiarly called, is read by over 40 percent of Austrians (3 million readers out of a 7.5 million population), making it one of the most popular newspapers in the world. Second, with a readership of almost 15 percent, is the *Kurier* daily paper. The German *WAZ* (*Westdeutsche Allgemeine Zeitung*) has a 45 percent stake in both.

German capital (in the shape of the Springer firm) also plays a role in the *Standard* newspaper, which started at

the end of the 1980s. Printed on salmon-pink paper, it is aimed at a liberal-intellectual readership.

The upper middle-class and conservative *Presse*, with its motto *Auch der Kopf braucht sein Frühstück* (literally: 'Give your brains some breakfast too'), is the city's second quality newspaper. Two other daily papers worth mentioning are the *Wiener Zeitung*, the official newspaper of the Austrian Republic, and the *Wirtschaffsblatt*, which focuses on economics.

The *Falter* was founded as a city magazine and, as a discussion forum, it is left-wing in its approach. It also contains the best 'What's On' guide. *City* is worthy in its approach and appeals to a chic, fashionable set. There are two English-language papers. One called *The Vienna Reporter* has been appearing every two weeks (with some interruptions) and carries news, events, etc; the other is a weekly called *Austria Today*.

Cultural events are also announced in the daily papers (especially in the Saturday editions).

Television & Radio

ORF, the Austrian radio and television concern monopolises the country's media and the political partie feel justified in intervening quite calml at the highest level where personne questions are involved. Quite often ministerial secretaries are given hig posts in the ORF, and vice-versa. To jobs at Tele 5, RTL and Premiere ar firmly in private hands.

The ORF has two TV stations (**F 1** and **FS 2**) and four radio station (**Ö1** with the emphasis on classical mu sic, **Ö2** with regional programmes, **Ö** with pop music, and also the foreign language station **FM4**, on 103.8 FM which carries news in English at 7am midday and 6pm. Private radio sta tions have discovered a few loophole recently – **Antenne Wien f.e.** or **88.6**, and **Radio Orange**.

Many homes in Vienna have cable TV, and a choice of more than two dozen channels.

POST & TELECOMMUNICATIONS

Most post offices are open Monday to Friday 8am–noon and 2–6pm (note that financial transactions can only take place until 5pm). The main post office in each of the districts is also open for two hours on Saturday morning, from 8am to 10am (again, no financial transactions).

Main Post Offices

Head Post Office: 1010, Fleischmarkt 19; daily 24 hours.
Postamt Börse: daily 24 hours
Südbahnhof: daily 24 hours
Westbahnhof: daily 24 hours
Franz-Josephs-Bahnhof: daily 24 hours
Airport: daily 7am–7.30pm

Telephoning

Phone boxes are plentiful in Vienna and invariably in good working order. They accept 1, 5, 10 and 20 *schilling* coins. Card phones are also widespread; phonecards can be purchased from post offices, kiosks, and other such outlets.

Dialling internationally is straightforward. The international access code from Austria is 00. After this, dial the relevant country code: Australia (61); Canada (1); Germany (49); Italy (39); Japan (81); the Netherlands (31); Spain (34); United Kingdom (44); United States (1).

If you are using a US phone credit card, dial the company's access number as follows: AT&T, tel: 022-903-011; MCI, tel: 022-903-012; Sprint, tel: 022-903-014.

SPECIAL SERVICES

Disabled People

CITY INFORMATION
(STADTINFORMATION)
1080, Rathaus (Town Hall; Entrance on Friedrich-Schmidt-Platz)
Tel: 525 50
Monday to Friday 8am–6pm

CLUB 21
1140, Linzerstrasse 466
Tel: 97 58 44 (Frau Nüchtern)
Monday to Friday 3–7pm

For Children

BÖRSE FUR PRIVATE KINDERBETREUUNG
Tel: 581 06 60-0/581 06 61-0
Monday, Wednesday, Friday 10am–4pm, Tuesday 10am–7pm, Thursday 8am–4pm

Open-air Swimming Pools for Children & Forest Playgrounds
Brochures detailing facilities can be obtained free of charge from Stadtinformation, 1080, Rathaus (Town Hall; entrance on Friedrich-Schmidt-Platz). Monday to Friday 8am–6pm, tel: 52550.
Swimming Pool Information Service: 601 120

HOLIDAY GAMES (FERIENSPIEL)
Tel: 4000 then dial 84400 direct (information)

RENAISSANCE THEATER
1070 Neubaug 38
Tel: 521 10–0

URANIA PUPPENSPIELE
(PUPPET THEATRE)
1010, Uraniastrasse 1
Tel: 712 61 91

NEU
LOTTO
Computer
6 aus 45
*Gewinn-
Garantie*

Pavement bingo

MOKI – MOBILE THEATRE FOR CHILDREN
1040, Blechturmgasse 12–13
Tel: 505 98 06

THEATER DER JUGEND
1070, Neubaugasse 38
Tel: 521 10–0

For Women

FRAUENCAFÉ
1080, Langegasse 11
Tel: 406 37 54

FRAUENHAUS
Tel: 545 48 00

Gays/Lesbians

AUTONOMES LESBENZENTRUM
1090, Währingerstrasse 59, Stiege VI
Tel: 408 50 57

HOSI – HOMOSEXUELLE INITIATIVE WIEN
1020, Novaragasse 40
Tel: 216 66 04
www.hosiwien.at
office@hosiwien.at

ROSA-LILA-VILLA
1060, Linke Wienzeile 102
Tel: 585 43 43

USEFUL ADDRESSES

Tourist Information

WIENER FREMDENVERKEHRSVERBAND
1025, Obere Augartenstrasse 40.
Tel: 211 14-0; Fax: 216 84 92
www.info.wien.at
Monday to Friday 8am–4pm
Those arriving in Vienna by car will find brochures, city maps and help in finding accommodation at the exits from the motorways: **Tourist Information Auhof/Wien West** at the exit ('Ausfahrt') from the Westautobahn A1; April to October daily 8am–10pm, January to March daily 10am–6pm.
Tourist Information Süd on the Südautobahn A2; at the exit marked Zentrum/Triesterstrasse; April to June and October: 9am–7pm, July to September 8am–10pm
Tourist Information at the Airport Arrivals Hall; January to May 8.30am–10pm, June to September 8.30am–11pm, October to December 9am–9pm
Tourist Information in the Centre Albertinaplatz, Vienna 1, daily 9am–7pm; tel: 513 88 92.
City Information (Stadtinformation) 1080, Town Hall, entrance on Friedrich-Schmidt-Platz, Tel: 525 50, Monday to Friday 8am–6pm
Austrobus: Opernpassage (between the exit 'Oper' and the exit 'Kärntnerstrasse'), daily 9am–7pm (provide information on hotels, currency exchange, theatre tickets, sightseeing tours, etc).

Overseas Information

AUSTRIAN TOURIST OFFICE
500 5th Avenue, #2009-2022
New York, NY 10110
Tel: 212 944 6885
Fax: 212 730 4568

AUSTRIAN TOURIST OFFICE
2 Bloor Street East, Suite 3330,
Toronto, Ontario
Tel: (416) 967 3381
Fax: (416) 967 4101

AUSTRIAN TOURIST OFFICE
14 Cork Street
London W1X 1PF
Tel: 020-7629 0461
Fax: 020-7499 6038

Travel Agencies

AMERICAN EXPRESS
1 Karntnerstrase 21–23
Tel: 515 110

COSMOS
1010, Kärntner Ring 15
Tel: 515 33 0

KUONI
1010, Wipplingerstrasse 34
Tel: 535 36 06

TUI
1010 Wipplingerstrasse 1
Tel: 535 41 55

RUEFA
1010, Rotenturmstrasse 20
Tel: 533 83 59

NECKERMANN ÖSTERREICH
1020 Lassallestrasse 7a
Tel: 502 02 0

ÖKISTA
1090 Garnisongasse 7 7
Tel: 401 48–0

Useful Numbers
Police: 133
Fire: 122
Ambulance: 144

Advance bookings
Bookings for the State Opera, the Volksoper and the Burgtheater can be made in writing to: Österreichischer Bundestheaterverband, Ticket Office, Hanuschgasse 3, Vienna. Credit cards, tel: 513 15 13.

FURTHER READING

History
Austria, Empire and Republic, by Barbara Jelavich (CUP).
Baroque and Rococo, edited by Anthony Blunt (Granada).
Dissolution of the Austro-Hungarian Empire, by J.W. Mason (Longman.)
The Fall of the House of Habsburg, by Edward Crankshaw.

The Habsburg Monarchy, by A.J.P. Taylor (Penguin, 1990).
Mayerling: the Facts behind the Legend, by Fritz Judtman (Harrap, 1971).
Nightmare in Paradise: Vienna and its Jews, by George E. Berkley (California University Press).

Art & Literature
The Age of the Baroque, 1610–1660, by Carl J. Friedrich (Greenwood Press, London).
Austrian Life and Literature – Eight Essays, edited by Peter Branscombe (Scottish Academic Press).
The Austrian Mind – An Intellectual and Social History 1848–1938, by William M. Johnstone (University of California Press).

Music Guide to Austria & Germany, by Elaine Brody (Dodd, 1975).
Looking for Mozart: a travel companion through Vienna (Salzburg and Prague), by Walter M. Weiss (Brandstaetter).
Vienna 1900 – Art, Architecture, Design, by Kirk Varnedoe.

General
Insight Guide: Vienna, Apa Publications, 2001.
Insight Guide: Austria, Apa Publications, 2001.
Insight Compact Guides: Salzburg and *Vienna*, Apa Publications, 2000

Fiction
The Third Man, by Graham Greene (Viking, 1950).

The U-bahn

Art & Photo Credits

front cover	**Peter Scholey/Stone**
Photography	**Nicole Schmidt** *and*
11	**Historisches Museum der Stadt Wien**
20	**J Klinger**
4, 16, 17, 18, 33, 40, 47, 51	**A Laudien**
12, 13, 30, 32, 36, 43, 49, 65, 67, 71, 77	**A Marcheselli**
back cover, 5	**Mark Read/APA**
18, 75, 80, 81, 87, 89	**Viennaslide**
21	**M O Weihs**
2/3 8/9, 63	**WFVV**
60	**WFVV-Markowitsch**
50	**WFVV-Mayer**
61	**WFVV-Simoner**
59	**WFVV-Wiesenhof**
38	**G Zugmann**
Illustration, page 52	**Martina Braun**
Designer	**Klaus Geisler**
Cover design	**Tanvir Virdee**
Cartography	**Berndtson & Berndtson**

INSIGHT
Pocket Guides

Insight Pocket Guides pioneered a new
approach to guidebooks, introducing the
concept of the authors as "local hosts" who
would provide readers with personal
recommendations, just as they would give
honest advice to a friend who came to stay.
They also included a full-size pull-out map.
Now, to cope with the needs of the 21st
century, new editions in this growing series
are being given a new look to make them
more practical to use, and restaurant and
hotel listings have been greatly expanded.

The travel guides
that replace a tour
guide – now better
than ever with
more listings and a
fresh new design

※ INSIGHT GUIDE

*The world's largest collection
visual travel guides*

*Now in
association
with*

Also from Insight Guides...

Insight Guides is the classic series, providing the complete picture with expert and informative text and stunning photography. Each book is an ideal travel planner, a reliable on-the-spot companion – and a superb visual souvenir of a trip. 193 titles.

Insight Maps are designed to complement the guidebooks. They provide full mapping of major destinations, and their laminated finish gives them ease of use and durability. 85 titles.

Insight Compact Guides are handy reference books, modestly priced yet comprehensive. The text, pictures and maps are all cross-referenced, making them ideal books to consult while seeing the sights. 119 titles.

INSIGHT POCKET GUIDE TITLES

Aegean Islands	California,	Israel	Moscow	Seville, Cordoba &
Algarve	Northern	Istanbul	Munich	Granada
Alsace	Canton	Jakarta	Nepal	Seychelles
Amsterdam	Chiang Mai	Jamaica	New Delhi	Sicily
Athens	Chicago	Kathmandu Bikes	New Orleans	Sikkim
Atlanta	Corsica	& Hikes	New York City	Singapore
Bahamas	Costa Blanca	Kenya	New Zealand	Southeast England
Baja Peninsula	Costa Brava	Kuala Lumpur	Oslo and	Southern Spain
Bali	Costa Rica	Lisbon	Bergen	Sri Lanka
Bali Bird Walks	Crete	Loire Valley	Paris	Sydney
Bangkok	Denmark	London	Penang	Tenerife
Barbados	Fiji Islands	Los Angeles	Perth	Thailand
Barcelona	Florence	Macau	Phuket	Tibet
Bavaria	Florida	Madrid	Prague	Toronto
Beijing	Florida Keys	Malacca	Provence	Tunisia
Berlin	French Riviera	Maldives	Puerto Rico	Turkish Coast
Bermuda	(Côte d'Azur)	Mallorca	Quebec	Tuscany
Bhutan	Gran Canaria	Malta	Rhodes	Venice
Boston	Hawaii	Manila	Rome	Vienna
Brisbane & the	Hong Kong	Marbella	Sabah	Vietnam
Gold Coast	Hungary	Melbourne	St. Petersburg	Yogjakarta
British Columbia	Ibiza	Mexico City	San Francisco	Yucatán Peninsula
Brittany	Ireland	Miami	Sarawak	
Brussels	Ireland's	Montreal	Sardinia	
Budapest	Southwest	Morocco	Scotland